# The Rise of the New Woman

# THE RISE OF THE NEW WOMAN

## The Women's Movement in America, 1875–1930

### Jean V. Matthews

*The American Ways Series*

IVAN R. DEE    *Chicago*

Library of Congress Cataloging-in-Publication Data:
Matthews, Jean V., 1937–
    The rise of the new woman : the women's movement in America, 1875–1930 / Jean V. Matthews.
        p. cm. — (The American ways series)
    Includes bibliographical references and index.
    ISBN 1-56663-500-4 (cloth : alk. paper) — ISBN 1-56663-501-2 (paper : alk. paper)
        1. Feminism—United States—History. 2. Women's rights—United States—History. I. Title. II. Series.

HQ1419 .M38 2003
305.42'0973—dc21                                                    2002035149

*For my husband*

# Contents

"Winning Plan." Racism and sexism. World War I and suffrage.
Passage of the Nineteenth Amendment.

# Acknowledgments

I WOULD LIKE to thank series editor John Braeman for helping clarify my thinking, and Ivan Dee for clarifying my prose. I also wish to thank the University of California at Berkeley Library, and the libraries of San Francisco State University and the University of San Francisco.

# The Rise of the New Woman

# 1

## The Woman's Era

I asked myself what was the most salient and peculiar point in
our social life. The answer was: the situation of women, the
decline of the sentiment of sex, the agitation on their behalf.
—Henry James, 1883

Do something, be of worth in yourself, form opinions, is the
imperative mood in which the times address modern women.
—"The Transitional American Woman," *Atlantic Monthly,* 1880

HENRY JAMES was not alone in seeing the problem
of women as the "most salient" feature of modern social life.
The journalist Kate Gannet Wells astutely recognized late-
nineteenth-century American women as both "transitional" and
"restless." California novelist Gertrude Atherton agreed: eight of
ten women, she claimed, were "possessed with an eager, restless
desire to be somebody, rise above the masses." She pointed to all
"the women who are writing, painting, journalizing, creeping
into public offices, and flocking to the stage." Even those without
any particular talent still wanted "to be independent, to strike
out for themselves, to be something more than domestic nonenti-
ties. These teach, telegraph, manipulate the type-writer, copy, become trained nurses, doctors. . . ." "All this," she added, "is the

result of the great women's rights agitation which has fastened its hooks about the axis of the earth."

Atherton exaggerated the causative role of the women's rights agitation; rather, that movement was itself a part of the new consciousness among a sizable portion of American women that the conditions of modern America both made possible—and even required—new fields of activity, a more active engagement with the wider world around them, even new modes of being.

The twenty years on either side of the turn of the twentieth century were a period of fundamental change and expansion in the roles and opportunities open to American women. The period culminated in the eventual success of a long drawn-out agitation for the vote, which seemed to bestow both formal recognition of equal citizenship and offer the opportunity for political power. In these forty years women had at least gained access to, and sometimes achieved substantial participation in, all levels of education, almost all the professions, a much wider range of jobs, and thus opportunities for some financial independence and a greater level of personal freedom. In the next fifty years it would become apparent that many doors were still effectively shut, and that much of the promise and appearance of equality was illusory, but to most middle-class women this earlier period offered a sense of progress and widening horizons.

This optimism was summed up in the *Woman's Century Calendar* issued by the National American Woman Suffrage Association at the beginning of the new century. It listed all the progressive developments for women over the course of the previous hundred years, from married women's property rights laws to the expansion of women's education. "The greatest achievement of the woman movement within the century," however, the *Calendar* proclaimed, was "the 'personal liberty' which is now conceded to women," the liberty "to do, to say, to go, and to be what one pleases, which has come to women." Not long ago "women in cities seen upon the streets devoted to business . . . were regarded with dark suspicion; now women are employed in every building on the business street, and a woman there excites no more comment than a man." Moreover, where once the mere idea of women organizing outside the home had seemed laughable or alarming, now there were literally thousands of women's organizations, with the total number of "organized women" nearing two million.

In pointing to the greater personal liberty and public visibility of women, the *Calendar* recognized how important it was that women with the opportunity to do so were moving out of domestic confinement. "Home," as Wells had noted rather disapprovingly, was "no longer the focus of *all* their endeavors.... The simple fact is that women have found that they can have occupation, respectability, and even dignity disconnected from the home." This did not mean that the ideology of domesticity and "separate spheres" had lost its normative and emotional impact. Indeed, the public encomiums to "Home" and woman's role within it grew louder as more women showed an inclination to escape its hold. The doctrine of "separate spheres" which had been worked out at the beginning of the nineteenth century, that men and women were designed by God and nature to operate in quite different arenas—men in the public world of exploit, war, work, intellect, and politics; women in the world of nurturance and the affections centered on the home—had offered an appealing solution for ordering the relations of the sexes in a modern liberal democracy. In effect it maintained the subordination of women without necessarily harping on their inferiority. It seemed to offer women their own autonomous space, and as long as they stayed there the culture showered them with fulsome compliments to "Woman" as the "Angel in the House," "Queen of the Home," the morally superior civilizer of men. Nevertheless the whole doctrine rested on the premise that women's lives were always ancillary to those of men, and that women should always be *dependent* on men.

Even before the Civil War a few women had begun to chafe against the constraints of "woman's sphere" and the assumption that nature had destined them to spend their lives as the behind-the-scenes support staff in the life drama of individually developing and achieving men. By 1848 a loosely organized "Woman's Rights" movement had sprung into existence, demanding for women full citizenship rights, including the right to vote, along with economic opportunities and access to all areas of modern life on an equality with men. A young upper-middle-class wife and mother, Elizabeth Cady Stanton, drew up the movement's manifesto: "We declare these rights to be self-evident, that all men *and women* are created equal."

After the Civil War the leaders of the movement had divided over a number of issues. The early activist Lucy Stone, who like most of the women's rights community had also been deeply involved in the anti-slavery movement, felt that women should not endanger passage of the Fifteenth Amendment, enfranchising the freedmen, by agitating to have it include women as well. Cady Stanton and her close colleague Susan B. Anthony adamantly refused to support a constitutional reform that further privileged men over women, and in 1869 they created a new organization, the National Woman Suffrage Association (NWSA), headquartered in New York, to pursue vigorously both suffrage and other women's issues. Stone and her husband Henry Blackwell retaliated with the American Woman Suffrage Association (AWSA) in Boston.

The two groups adopted different plans of organization and different strategies in their campaigns for suffrage, but more important were differences of style and willingness to take up issues of sexuality and marriage. Conservatives had always connected the emancipation of women with sexual promiscuity, and Lucy Stone was disturbed by Cady Stanton's persistent championing of easier divorce laws. She was also horrified by the scandal in the early 1870s caused by the NWSA's brief alliance with the flamboyant prophetess of Free Love, Victoria Woodhull. Stone feared, with much justification, that all this would provide lethal ammunition to the movement's enemies and frighten off the mass of conservative and traditional women. The AWSA would campaign for suffrage and champion new opportunities for women but carefully avoid anything that might impugn its respectability.

By the 1880s, however, both organizations were steering clear of any attempt to examine marriage as an institution that confined women, or anything that might be construed as an attack on religion, the churches, or conventional sexual morality. As the titles of the two associations indicate, the vote, which had been but one of the many goals of the prewar movement, now assumed the central role.

The idea of women as voters was controversial enough, for it challenged the basic tenet of "separate spheres" that women's relations with the world outside the home were rightly mediated by the "protection" and representation of husbands and fathers. Enfranchised women would have a direct and independent connection to the state as individuals, quite apart from their vital but subordinate situation as a member of a family, and would speak in their own voice, not through another. However "restless" women were becoming, only a small minority as yet were prepared to make a public declaration for equality and proclaim themselves adherents of "women's rights." Nonetheless the challenge had been made and did not go away; the ridicule or horrified denunciations of its opponents, as much as the dedication of its defenders, helped keep it in the public eye. As women began to move into new spheres of activity, the mere existence of an articulate "women's rights" movement made available an ideology that could explain these separate developments as aspects of one grand movement of women toward equality with men.

Many of the changes in women's lives could be summed up less controversially under the blanket term "the advancement of women," a sufficiently vague phrase that was mildly progressive yet safe. Many women who might hesitate to go to a women's rights meeting would happily attend a lecture under the auspices of the American Association for the Advancement of Women

(AAAW, founded in 1873) on such topics as higher education for women or promoting the "financial independence of women." Attendance at the annual conferences, held in a different city each year, ran into the thousands, and newspapers respectfully reported the proceedings. Some prominent members, like Julia Ward Howe, the revered author of the "Battle Hymn of the Republic" who became its president in 1881, were suffragists, but the association as a whole carefully avoided the subject. Two young women who went to an 1875 meeting of the AAAW in Syracuse, New York, recalled that they had settled into their seats with "a sense of surrender to the forces of expansion and progress."

Many of women's expansive possibilities had to do with the rapid growth of American cities in the post–Civil War era. In 1870, 14 cities could boast a population of more than 100,000; by 1900 there were 38. While most Americans lived on the land until 1920, urban areas were attracting more and more newcomers, both the native-born from the farms and foreign immigrants, seeking a better life. "There are great cities," confided the 17-year-old future temperance leader Frances Willard to her diary, in an aspiration shared by many young rural and small-town girls, "but I'm not in one!—but I *will* be."

Foreign visitors were struck by the sheer numbers of women on city streets. The establishment of great department stores by the 1870s created a new pleasurable public space that was largely female, and the development of public transport—commuter trains and streetcars—enabled women to travel into and around town by themselves. By the late 1880s major city streets were lit at night, making them safer and more comfortable for women. "The increase in the number of women abroad at night, with no other protector than the benign beams of the electric light," remarked one commentator in 1896, "affords a new and interesting manifestation of the streets."

After the Civil War the theater became more respectable, and in the 1870s managers saw the opportunity offered by the new freedom of women in public and instituted matinees, which women could attend unescorted by a man. Women's taste was now often controlling in what made a theatrical success, just as the woman reader was becoming the key in making a best-selling book. The last quarter of the nineteenth century was also the great age of the actress. The major stars were female—women like the statuesque beauty Lillian Russell and the young Ethel Barrymore. The development of photography allowed their images to be widely spread via magazines, or displayed in shop windows, to achieve a greater popular recognition than most public men. Their private lives were reported on, their opinions sought. They were conspicuous examples of women who made a good deal of money by their own talents and used it to lead independent and glamorous lives.

By the 1880s too, the lecture circuit was flourishing, part of the educational and entertainment activities of most middle-class people. Women speakers, who in the years before the Civil War had caused such a scandal, were now welcome and well paid. Women even began to invade the world of news reportage. When in 1889 Joseph Pulitzer of the *New York World* decided to send a reporter around the world in less than the eighty days of Jules Verne's recent novel hero, he chose a twenty-two-year-old "girl reporter," Nellie Bly. The stunt would not have had such an impact if he had dispatched a man. Nellie Bly symbolized both the new mobility and the new visibility of women outside the home.

In cities, the wonders of the new industrial economy were most evident—along with its accompanying social problems. The new mansions of a new class of the superrich were tokens of a lifestyle of luxurious display more flamboyant than anything Americans had witnessed. The burgeoning slums that housed a largely immigrant population of the working poor were a separate world. But the cities and towns were also home to a rapidly expanding middle class, and it was on the whole to women of this class that the possibilities for "advancement" appealed most strongly. To the core of business owners, professionals, and prosperous farmers that had constituted the prewar middle class was now added a growing number of white-collar salaried men working in large businesses and corporations, plus new professionals like accountants, managers, civil engineers, newspapermen, and academics to augment the traditional core of clergy, lawyers, and doctors. From the clerk to the prosperous lawyer there was a quite large range of income, but this expanding middle class was distinguished by its "white-collar" occupations and by a self-conscious gentility. It was the class that was most committed to an ideal of respectable domesticity and to separate spheres—but it also produced the committed rebels against that ideology, as well as the women who were making tentative steps outside the home.

It was among this middle class too that the concept of the "lady," involving an increasingly restrictive code of etiquette as to how a woman should behave and how she should be treated, had the greatest influence. The codes of ladydom were the means by which middle-class women ranked and judged each other and which governed and rendered stiff and uneasy the relations between the sexes. On the assumption that all relations between men and women, particularly young ones, were potentially sexual in nature, they had to be hedged about with external and internalized prohibitions to protect the purity—and thus marriageability—of young women. Women of the expanding middle class found themselves caught between a new urban freedom, with its promise of privacy and even self-determination, and a more oppressive code of conduct governing the deportment of the "lady," which few dared to flout. By the turn of the century a growing number of women would rebel against the bonds of ladydom; yet for most women, including increasingly working-class and African-American women, the status of "lady," which became a moral as much as a social designation, was their main claim to consideration.

One of the marks of the middle class was its high valuation of education, not just for its sons but increasingly for its daughters too. By the 1880s a new female type had emerged—the formally educated woman with a high school diploma or even a college degree in hand to prove it. All movements for female emancipation begin with calls to close the education gap between men and women. Young women's yearning for educational opportunities on a par with their brothers had been strong before the Civil War, but the real breakthrough came after the war, with a great expansion in the creation of public, usually coeducational, high schools and in the number and size of colleges.

Even by 1900 graduation from high school remained very much a minority achievement; still, the number of teenagers enrolled climbed from less than 2 percent in 1870 to more than 5 percent by the turn of the century—and of these, 57 percent were girls. The old traditional colleges of the Eastern states had always been, and remained, for men only, but new institutions in the West and Midwest were either coeducational from the beginning or quickly became so, and so were most new postwar Eastern universities outside the South. In 1870 fewer than 1 percent of young Americans went to college, but women already made up 21 percent of those students; by 1890 they were just under 36 percent of a much larger student body, and by 1920 nearly half. Female undergraduates still represented a small percentage of American women, but by 1900 there were already 85,000 of them, almost entirely from the broad middle class. In some cases parents made considerable financial sacrifices to educate their daughters; in others young women paid their own way by scrimping and saving the salaries they had earned as teachers.

Many older women were prepared to organize, petition, and fund-raise to give the younger generation of women the opportunities they had not had themselves. Ezra Cornell's decision to make his foundation coeducational owed much to the pressure of Elizabeth Cady Stanton and Susan B. Anthony, and the University of Rochester only reluctantly agreed to admit women in 1900 after the city's women had painfully raised $100,000 to pay for the transition. The patronage of wealthy women was also important. At Berkeley, Phoebe Hearst, wife of Senator George Hearst, gave scholarship money for young women and funds to hire Berkeley's first woman faculty member. At Johns Hopkins, women were accepted into the new medical school only because a wealthy heiress offered the university a large sum of money on that condition.

At least in the early years there remained a good deal of resentment among some male faculty and students against women "coeds," for the men feared that their degrees would be cheapened if they could also be won by women. Many male students also saw women as intruders into male sociability, disrupting the close camaraderie they particularly valued in their college experience, and by their mere presence as "ladies" inevitably putting a damper on male high spirits. Women at coeducational colleges and universities seem to have taken for granted their somewhat marginal status, or perhaps not quite realized how marginal it was, until some unexpected slight brought it home to them. "There was no prejudice against women students," one alumna of Berkeley declared stoutly, but added that it had been a painful surprise "to aim for a Phi Beta Kappa key, only to learn that there would be no girls on the list because when it came to finding a good job, men needed the help of this honor more than women did."

In the new women's colleges founded after the Civil War, however, the female student was on home ground: she did not need to feel that she was an interloper trespassing on male turf. These separate colleges—Vassar (1865), Wellesley and Smith (1875), and Bryn Mawr (1884)—were founded out of an ideological commitment to the higher education of women as such. Smith was founded by a wealthy widow; Vassar, Wellesley, and Bryn Mawr were all creations of individual wealthy and devout men who came out of the prewar abolitionist, evangelical, and reform milieus. All the founders saw themselves as emancipators—Matthew Vassar compared himself to Lincoln. Henry F.

Durant, the founder of Wellesley, declared that "the higher Education of Women is one of the great world battle-cries for freedom. . . . It is the assertion of absolute equality."

The first generation of women college students was acutely aware that they were pioneers and that their lapses or failures might jeopardize the whole "experiment" of higher education for women. They felt that "all the world was breathlessly watching," recalled a Wellesley alumna, class of 1879. By the end of the century the idea of women in college was more taken for granted. In 1890 even the conservative *Ladies Home Journal* offered a four-year scholarship to Vassar, Wellesley, or Smith to the girl who could sell the most subscriptions to the magazine. The woman college graduate would come to have an impact and visibility in public life beyond her actual numbers. When a *Woman's Who's Who in America* was published in 1914 (in itself a significant indication of the growing public life of women), 43.8 percent of those listed had college degrees, 52 percent among women under fifty. Among single women in the directory, 40 percent had attended professional or graduate school. The separate women's colleges were particularly notable in the disproportionate number of their graduates who went on to distinguished careers in the professions and social reform.

By the turn of the century, magazines and newspapers were filled with discussions of a new type of female personality: the "New Woman." The actual term seems to have been coined around 1894, but the type was instantly recognizable and the name immediately caught on. As a type, the New Woman was young, well educated, probably a college graduate, independent of spirit, highly competent, and physically strong and fearless. The avatar of the New Woman was the so-called Gibson Girl, named for her creator, the artist Charles Dana Gibson, who began to draw her for *Life* magazine in the 1890s. Her imperious image appeared everywhere, often shown wearing what became the uniform of the New Woman: a high-collared, rather severe white shirtwaist blouse, tucked into a plain dark skirt. The skirt stopped at the ankles and was neither full and beruffled nor so narrow that it was difficult to walk. It was in fact very much an all-purpose outfit; though some women wore bloomers or divided skirts to ride the new bicycles, in fact it was quite possible to ride in the new skirt, as well as hike and go camping, or even climb mountains—other favorite pastimes of the New Woman.

The shirtwaist costume imparted an appearance of brisk competence and was adopted not only by the upper-middle-class New Woman but by the girls who were flocking into business as office workers. The shirtwaist was part of the revolution taking place in the production of clothing; it was one of the first articles of women's dress to be mass produced and made available readymade. Like much mass-produced clothing, it could be democratically available quite far down the social scale, because the women who made these fashions in factories or small sweatshops were paid very low wages.

The physical freedom of the New Woman was evident not just in her dress but in her athleticism. By the end of the century, women were playing tennis, golf, and basketball; they went sailing, swimming, skating, and bowling. And they were riding bicycles—one of the insignia of the New Woman. Since it was impossible to ride a bicycle sidesaddle, this was an activity that men and women not only engaged in together but did in much the same way. An 1891 Boston editorial remarked how startling it was to see "young girls from the best families . . . whirling through the public thoroughfares, like so many boys," and described how a young doctor and his bride had gone off on their honeymoon trip to California, each mounted on a bicycle. "However little she may realize it," the writer concluded, "every girl who rides her steel horse is a vivid illustration of one of the greatest waves of progress of this century, the advancement of women in freedom and opportunity."

Perhaps even more significant than the mobility and educational attainments of young women was the organizational activity of the middle-aged. The *Woman's Calendar* had seized upon it as a signal mark of progress. Hundreds of new women's "clubs" were formed after the Civil War, enrolling thousands of women. Unlike the pre–Civil War sewing circles, these clubs were not under clerical auspices nor devoted to charity; unlike the abolitionist and women's rights organizations, they were not radical fringe groups. They deliberately used the male term "club" to indicate a new kind of venture for women, more formal and impersonal than most existing women's circles. Many clubs actually forbade members to bring sewing or knitting to do during discussions.

The first object of almost all the clubs was intellectual self-improvement. The members met to study and enlarge their minds; they were women who had not had the opportunities for higher education that were opening up for their daughters' generation. Although most clubs were fairly small, many, especially in larger cities, grew to memberships of over five hundred, and then would be divided into departments, each concentrating on a particular area of interest—literature, art, history, education, and, increasingly, civic improvement. Many towns eventually owed their public library to the women's clubs. Small clubs met in members' parlors, but the larger ones rented public rooms, and by the 1890s some were even building their own clubhouses.

Middle-class women could form and attend these clubs because they had a certain amount of leisure and almost always some domestic help. Even more important than the availability of servants, however, was the decline in the birthrate. Between 1860 and 1910 the number of children per white woman dropped from just over five to just under three and a half. The decline was most noticeable among the native-born and the middle class. For African-American women, too, the birthrate declined by about one-third. This meant that by the time she was middle-aged a woman probably no longer had children at home who needed constant attention. Coupled with the fact that, unlike the farmer, the urban husband did not need to be fed at noon, this left the married woman the possibility of an afternoon at leisure.

The great majority of clubwomen were not only middle and upper middle class but white and Protestant, and by no means immune to the endemic racism and anti-Semitism of the period; very few clubs welcomed either Jewish or African-American women. Experiencing the same drive toward organization and self-development, both these groups created separate club movements. Josephine St. Pierre Ruffin, an upper-class Boston woman, started one of the first African-American clubs. Activated by the same buoyant feeling that a new age was dawning for women, it called itself the New Era Club, publishing a journal entitled *Woman's Era*.

In 1892 a General Federation of Women's Clubs was formed, with some 100,000 members; by 1910 membership was almost a million. The Federation held biennial conferences in different locations across the country attended by hundreds of delegates; railroads offered half-fare "convention rates" to get them there, and the press gave extensive coverage. The opposition of Southern members meant that no African-American clubs would be accepted into the General Federation, and in 1895 they federated into their own National Association of Colored Women. By this time the woman's club was clearly a formidable presence in American life.

The study clubs did not exhaust the seemingly inexhaustible urge to organize: the Daughters of the American Revolution, the Daughters of the Confederacy, and the Colonial Dames were all post–Civil War organizations to proclaim class status and to appropriate the glories of the American past for women as for men. For rural women it was harder to organize on their own, but when the new farmers' groups like the Grange and the Farmers' Alliance encouraged them to join, women responded. Working-class women also organized clubs, asserting their own right to make time for study, to prove that "we can and do think," that they too were "capable of self-determination and worthy of respect." By 1897 a coordinating body, the National League of

Women Workers, had been formed, and in 1914 it had 14,000 members and affiliates in major cities across the country.

Members of women's clubs from the most activist to the most conservative seem to have had an acute awareness of themselves as pioneers in a new way of life for women. They had a sense of their own organizational history and what membership meant in their lives, particularly in the experience of gradually growing accustomed "to the sound of their own voices." Club members acquired the self-confidence to speak in a public group, to participate in the give-and-take of discussion outside the family circle. The clubs thus saw themselves as agents of self-culture in the most basic sense, not merely as means for acquiring culture but, more important, as agents of personal growth and transformation.

Among the most successful of women's organizations were the new women's mission boards. The great surge in foreign mission activity among the Protestant churches from the 1880s to World War I depended heavily on the independent activity of women as fund-raisers and missionaries. The first separate women's mission board was founded in 1869; by 1900 there were forty-one American women's boards, and by 1915 more than three million women were members of foreign mission societies. Like secular women's organizations, the mission societies gave women the opportunity for leadership and for developing organizational skills. Nervous clergymen insisted that women remember that leadership in church enterprises was a male prerogative, but women zealously guarded and defended their independent activities. As one Methodist activist declared militantly: "I propose to open every door that the Lord sets before me, as a member of the Woman's Christian Temperance Union, or the Woman's Foreign Missionary Society . . . or anything else. Anywhere with Jesus, everywhere with Jesus; and put all my prejudices behind and march on to victory."

Women had always constituted the silent backbone of American religion, but now restless women were becoming increasingly dissatisfied with established religious avenues. They were searching for new spiritual paths, like Spiritualism, that provided them with greater independence and power. The challenge to male authority was even more direct in the extraordinary figure of Mary Baker Eddy, who in her fifties found her vocation as the new messiah. The victim—like apparently many other American women of the time—of various nervous and other ills, she had been cured not by conventional medicine but by a "mental healer." From this experience Eddy developed the "Science of divine metaphysical healing," which, as expounded in her 1875 book *Science and Health,* became the bible of a new religion: Christian Science.

Eddy was a brilliant organizer and businesswoman, and by 1906 she could count about 85,000 acknowledged Christian Scientists. The numbers and wealth of the church would continue to grow through the middle of the twentieth century, the handsome neoclassical church and the Christian Science reading room becoming prominent features of most towns. To its adherents the new religion offered the promise of perfect health and the power to control one's own destiny through the power of thought. In this lay much of its special appeal to women, who felt themselves to be among the powerless in society, without control even over their own bodies.

Christian Science was but one, though the most successful and institutionalized, of a whole range of ideas popularly known as New Thought, a shifting and rather fuzzy amalgam of ideas from Eastern religions, self-healing, and the power of thought to achieve individual desires. Optimistic and eclectic, New Thought feminized the deity and gave women a particularly direct pipeline to spiritual reality. Indeed, New Thought made "Woman" central to a new vision of the future, when the powers "of muscle and sword and bullet" and the chaos created by unrestrained ruthless masculine competition would soon be replaced by a new spiritual power based on the morality and selfless purity of women. Thus the belief in the power of the mind over circumstances offered the individual woman the possibility of self-transformation and suggested that women as a sex could lead in ushering in a new and better world.

Many women were becoming critical of the new industrial society that men had made, even as they benefited from its bounty. A special target was its ruthless competitiveness, driving the weakest to the wall; this seemed a prime example of the effects of uncontrolled masculine aggression. Socialism, which probably reached the height of its influence in America between the 1880s and World War I, appealed to many activist women, particularly in the nonrevolutionary, gradualist, and/or Christian Social Gospel variety taken up by many progressive men. Women were the majority of adherents of the "Nationalist" movement that flourished briefly in the wake of Edward Bellamy's hugely successful utopian novel, *Looking Backward* (1887), which offered a vision of a rigidly organized but peaceful cooperative society with abundance for all and equality between men and women.

The most successful organization of the period in bringing large numbers of women into organized activity and transforming many was the Women's Christian Temperance Union (WCTU), founded in 1874. Devoted at first to encouraging temperance on an individual basis, the organization quickly converted to agitating for state prohibition of the sale of liquor. Under the inspired leadership of Frances Willard, its president from 1879 to 1898, the WCTU spread rapidly across the country in the 1880s. By 1892 the WCTU had at least 150,000 members and its newspaper, the *Union Signal*, reached a circulation of almost 100,000. Organized into local chapters under a national federation, the WCTU combined considerable local autonomy with national direction.

Frances Willard was a college graduate who had been briefly dean of women at Northwestern University and was deeply committed to the "woman movement" even before turning her attention to temperance as her life's work. One of the most

charismatic women of her generation, she was a dynamic re-
cruiter and organizer. With a genius for the inspiring slogan,
Willard made the motto of the WCTU "Home Protection." This
echoed a major political issue of the time—free trade versus protective tariffs—and converted it into an issue of decisive interest
to women. Drunkenness was, after all, viewed as a basic threat to
the home, and the saloon, a separate social world of men, was the
home's prime rival for male resources. Male violence triggered
by drink and male wages squandered in the saloon could destroy
the basis for woman's domestic role as well as her security and
that of her children. In defense of their "sphere" and their children, generally conventional and religious women could be led
beyond prayers to political action, though most temperance
women initially were anxious not to be classified with the
"strong-minded," who were demanding equality with men and
the right to vote.

Willard assured the world, and women recruits themselves,
that what activated women who joined the WCTU was "Not
Rights, but Duties." "Duty" was a much used word in the public
pronouncements of women trying to urge other women into a
more active public life, and a word that most women felt far
more comfortable with than "rights." Rights implied unfeminine
self-assertion, likely to arouse strong male opposition and, even
worse, ridicule. "Duty," on the other hand, presented itself as a
*command* that women could only obey, and was hard to quarrel
with. In terms of practical effects, however, "rights" and "duties"
tended to lead in much the same direction: out of the home and
into the world.

By 1896 the WCTU had thirty-nine different national departments, many of which had no direct connection at all with temperance but were related to the general well-being and interests
of women and children: agitation and support for compulsory
education laws, prison reform and child labor legislation, investigation of the causes of alcoholism, and temperance teaching in
public schools. The organization had quickly spread to other

countries, and by 1884 there was a World's WCTU with an ambitious goal of the complete worldwide suppression of liquor,
opium, and prostitution. Willard described these goals slightly
differently as "the blessed trinity of movements"—prohibition,
the uplift of labor, and "woman's liberation."

The white ribbon, which the members of the WCTU adopted
as their badge, symbolized not only temperance but a whole vision of a purified society. It led its members into demanding such
public amenities as school baths and public drinking fountains,
on the one hand, and censorship of a great variety of "objection-
able" media, on the other. In 1883 the WCTU created a Department for the Suppression of Impure Literature and took on
"immoral" books and magazines along with theater, ballet,
prizefighting, gambling, and, by the turn of the century, movies.
Unlike many of the other expansive departments of the WCTU,
this one survived Willard's death in 1898 and became particularly active in the 1920s.

The WCTU's concern with "purity" was part of a larger
movement for stricter sexual and moral standards that the histo-
rian David Pivar has dubbed the "Purity Crusade," in which
women were especially prominent. One of the prime goals was to
eliminate prostitution. To the acutely self-conscious women of
the late nineteenth century, the very existence of the prostitute
undermined the moral status of womanhood in general and was
a humiliating symbol of woman as existing only for the "use" of
men. In the 1880s the WCTU also undertook several successful
campaigns to raise the "age of consent"—thirteen or below in the
majority of states; by 1894 the average age of consent had been
raised to fourteen.

Attacks on prostitution slid easily into attacks on the sexual
double standard, an issue that stirred women from the most conservative to the most radical, and pointed to sexuality as the main
contested terrain between men and women. Not that women
cared to share the sexual laxity of men; rather, they wanted to
make men conform to the sexual standards demanded of

women, and this meant men's sexual conduct inside marriage as
well as out. The violence of drunken husbands against wives that
the WCTU was constantly denouncing included sexual violence
and the unwelcome pregnancies that might result. The fact that
the birthrate was declining indicates considerable cooperation
here among husbands and wives, but the widespread indignation
this whole issue raised also suggests that women often lost out in
marital negotiation on sex.

The sexual fears of white women affected their response to
one of the greatest brutalities of the age: lynching. Between 1880
and 1930 some 3,220 African-American men were lynched in
the South, often on the charge of rape or attempted rape of a
white woman. In 1893 Willard actually persuaded the WCTU to
pass an anti-lynching resolution, but at the same time she condemned "the unspeakable outrages which have so often pro-
voked such lawlessness," and on speaking tours in the South she
sympathized with Southern white women's fears of black men.
She was angrily taken to task for this by the outspoken African-
American journalist Ida B. Wells of Memphis, who had
launched a one-woman crusade against lynching. Wells had already violated the most basic of American taboos in suggesting
publicly that, not only was the charge of rape often trumped up,
but that if sex had taken place it was quite likely consensual, and
even initiated by the white woman. On a speaking tour in England, Wells sharply denounced Willard for her unthinking acceptance as fact of the charge that lynching was a response to
sexual threats to white women. Willard was embarrassed by the
rebuke but did not retract her remarks. Wells was never able to
get any of the women's organizations to take up the issue of
lynching. The general racist climate, combined with the sexual
fear of many white women, made them unwilling to speak out
against a practice that, however brutally, they felt "protected"
them. Not until 1930 would the former suffragist Jessie Daniel
Ames be able to organize Southern women to take a public stand
against lynching.

Willard was also a suffragist. By 1881 she had brought the national convention of the WCTU to endorse votes for women, as
women began to realize their own lack of real power to bring
about prohibition. After her death many rank-and-file members
retreated from this exposed position, though others made the
crossover from apprenticeship in the temperance cause to becoming suffrage activists. The Mississippian Belle Kearney ascribed
her own journey from conventional Southern daughter to suffrage worker and the first woman elected to the Mississippi Senate to her involvement with the WCTU. It was, she said, "the
Golden key that unlocked the prison doors of pent-up possibilities."

The success of the WCTU in mobilizing women far surpassed that of the organized suffrage movement, mainly because
it did not directly challenge the concept of separate spheres.
What gave the WCTU, like the club and other women's organizations, a revolutionary potential, however, was the mere fact
that they were conscious components of what the women themselves came to call "organized womanhood." When women organized themselves as a sex they were forging an identity and
networks of affiliation that were outside the little world of the
family, which was the heart of woman's "separate sphere." They
were asserting that as women they had interests as a sex that they
could not rely on men to defend, or express, for them. They had
a right to speak for themselves in society, the church, and even
the state. The suffragist Mary Livermore grasped the emancipatory potential when she insisted that it was not "a mere blind
craze that is sweeping women into clubs and leagues. . . . It is the
trend of the age; an unconscious protest against the isolation in
which women have dwelt in the past; a reaching out after a
larger and fuller life; a desire to keep in touch with other women
who are thinking and acting independently; it is a necessary step
in the evolution of women." Former president Grover Cleveland
saw what was happening too when he nervously warned women
in 1904 against the insidious "club habit." "The best and safest

club for a woman to patronize," he insisted solemnly, "is her home."

The growth of "organized womanhood" was a hopeful development for the woman suffrage movement, since these were women who were already emancipating themselves from domestic confinement and should be ready for conversion to a more ideological attack on the subordination of women. Yet the many organizations, and particularly the WCTU, were rivals for the allegiance and energies of "restless" women. The task facing the suffrage leaders was to position the suffrage movement as the advance guard in the "evolution of women" and to persuade and push women toward the goal of full and equal citizenship symbolized by the vote.

At this they were not having much success. There are no precise membership figures for the two suffrage associations, but they were certainly small. The decision by leaders in both organizations to concentrate their energies on the vote alone may have been counterproductive. With such a small membership it seemed that they could not afford to dissipate their forces by taking on other issues or risk losing members by, as Susan B. Anthony said, arousing their "whims and prejudices on other subjects." Some activists certainly thought this was a mistaken strategy. Clara Colby, a longtime activist and editor of a rather quirky suffrage newspaper, gave an impassioned plea for new thinking at the 1886 NWSA convention. "Why is it," she demanded "that the woman suffrage movement does not force itself as a vital issue into the thoughts of the masses?" Somehow the movement was missing the "connecting link between the abstract right on which we stand and the common heart and sympathy which must be enlisted for our cause ere it can succeed." She thought Frances Willard offered a valuable lesson to suffragists in how to appeal to the average woman. "It is the practical bearings of the movement that have led the marshalled hosts of the White Ribbon army to give it their hand," she insisted. "Women who draw back cold and scornful when spoken to of the abstract right to the ballot and the fundamental necessity for the equality of the sexes, pledge themselves to effort when Frances Willard points out the value of the ballot as a temperance weapon." Suffragists needed to "vitalize" the movement, and one way to do so, Colby told her colleagues, was to align themselves with the interests of working women and their problems of economic and social injustice.

While there were often fairly ritualistic expressions of concern about the problems of working women among suffragists, during these years there seems to have been little real effort by the suffrage organizations to draw them in. When a group of working women attempted to gain the floor at the 1880 NWSA convention in Chicago, they appear to have been snubbed. Nor did the movement ever try to capitalize on a real strain of barely repressed anger among many housewives below the status of the clubwomen. In 1880 Anthony organized an (unsuccessful) campaign to persuade the Republican party to put woman suffrage on its platform, and appealed to women who could not attend the meeting in Chicago at least to send a postcard expressing support on the issue. She received several thousand letters, often with multiple signatures, and many of them seething with resentment.

One "old lady" from Iowa was still resentful that her illiterate mother had sent her brothers to school because *they* needed an education to "go out in the world smart men" while keeping her at home to work. "Let them know you mean freedom if we never get it keep them stirred up that is some satisfaction," she urged Anthony. "Have seen man's cruelty to women many times; just because they delighted to show their power over them. It must be stopped. . . . I hope the time is coming when the women can put their foot down heavy on any man that dares to trample on their rights" (Illinois); ". . . withholding from feminine humanity every natural right from infancy to death, is man's natural propensity. . . . am bitter enough if it comes to that, to fight manfully for our liberty" (Kansas); "i have a desire to vote. . . .

when will we have our Rights and Justice in this world."
(Philadelphia); ". . . the condition of the farmers and their poor
drudging wives, is every year becoming more intolerable. . . . do
I want to vote; yes, I do, and I would like to be Robertspere . . . til
the head of every murderer and every sin-licensing states-man
had rolled down from the guillotine" (Minnesota); "We are your
Sister though Colored. . . . Our White men of this State of Virginia . . . rule us with a rod of iron" (Virginia).

Here was a potentially explosive mix of angry emotions that
might have been galvanized into a mass popular base for suffrage, just as the Populist movement was able to do for its program. But no one among the suffrage leaders, even the most
radical, knew what to do with this kind of anger.

A new leadership group had joined the suffrage cause after
the Civil War, women who came to women's rights in midlife
and out of the experience of the war years rather than from the
old anti-slavery crusade, and when the question of women voting, though still highly contentious, was no longer quite so outrageous as it had seemed in the 1850s. Women like Mary
Livermore of Chicago, who had been a prominent organizer in
the Sanitary Commission during the war, and Julia Ward Howe
bestowed a new prestige on the movement, but they also served
to keep the lid on any socially radical tendencies.

The new women leaders were more comfortable in playing
down conflicts of interest between men and women or between
classes, and insisting that women's political emancipation would
bring social harmony because of women's more disinterested and
nurturing nature. Nor would the franchise in any way disrupt
the home or the position of women within it. Elizabeth Harbert,
a journalist and clubwoman, president of the Illinois suffrage association from 1876, and active in the NWSA, was fairly typical
of this ideological direction. In her newspaper column, like the
WCTU she emphasized "duties" rather than rights, and based
women's claims to greater power on their duties and capacities as
mothers. "Our hour for self-sacrificing service is here," she pro-

claimed in 1885, thus capitulating to the cultural prescription—and the general female desire to believe—that the good woman never acted on behalf of "self" but only of others.

Like most clubwomen, the suffragist organizations also distanced themselves from African-American women. This was partly due again to the growing number of women in the movement who had not been part of its anti-slavery antecedents. The distance the movement had traveled from its early roots in anti-slavery can be seen in a revealing statement by the Indiana suffragist May Wright Sewell, who in 1885 suggested that for the first time the annual NWSA convention be held in a Southern city. The movement needed to reach out to white women in the South, she explained, to overcome the perception that woman suffrage was "as much a form of Northern fanaticism as abolition was."

For white women, as for white men, reconciliation with the white South meant abandonment of African Americans and a slide toward accepting the white Southern attitude on race relations. Once the suffrage movement leaders had made a commitment to recruit Southern white women, they found themselves continually making compromises on race questions so as not to offend Southern sensibilities. In private, Anthony could still wax indignant over issues of race discrimination, but she nevertheless asked the distinguished black orator Frederick Douglass, who had been a pillar of the women's rights movement since 1848, not to attend the 1895 convention in Atlanta and take his usual prominent place on the platform. She steadfastly refused to allow issues of discrimination—like the barring of black women from the "ladies" car on Southern railroads, which was extremely important to the growing class of educated and organized African-American women—to be introduced into the suffrage organizations. White women's rights organizations from now on would refuse to acknowledge the linkage between racism and sexism, despite the continued efforts of African-American women to make them do so.

The African-American educator Anna Julia Cooper, in her 1892 *A Voice from the South*, charged that white women bore a particular responsibility for racism. Civility was a basic civic virtue, since it provided the essential basis for a republic of treating all people with dignity and respect. Through their influence over manners and morals, Cooper was convinced that white women had the power to modify the pervasive vicious racial prejudice; yet they refused to use it, either because they feared to, because they shared such prejudice, or from sheer thoughtlessness. Cooper took the suffrage orator Anna Howard Shaw sharply to task for a speech in which she had tried to rouse opinion in favor of votes for women by denouncing as outrageous the proposal to extend voting rights to Indian men. "The Reform of our day, known as the Woman's Movement," insisted Cooper, "is essentially such an embodiment, if its pioneers could only realize it, of the universal good. And specially important is it that there be no confusion of ideas among its leaders as to its scope and universality."

By the 1880s the two rival but in many ways complementary suffrage organizations had settled into a steady and largely unsuccessful routine of working for the vote. In 1878 Senator A. A. Sargent of California introduced a federal amendment, drafted by Elizabeth Cady Stanton, which at that time would have been the Sixteenth—though in the event it ended up as the Nineteenth: "The right of citizens of the United States to vote shall not be denied or abridged by the United States or by any state on account of sex." The proposal was ritually reintroduced year after year in the 1880s, once even coming to a vote in the Senate, where it was defeated 34 to 16, with 26 absent. After 1896 it was not discussed in Congress again until 1913. The AWSA concentrated on a different approach of working for the vote in each state separately. Between 1874 and 1890, seven states held referenda on women's suffrage, and all were heavily defeated.

In the late 1870s Stanton and Anthony took time out from active organizing to compile a history of their movement. Anthony

had saved a good deal in the way of letters, speeches, and newspaper clippings for just such a project, and she enlisted all the fellow workers she could to search for records. The enormous
collection of original documents they compiled—of reminis-
cences, letters, speeches, newspaper articles, and convention
records—eventually grew into three volumes, published in 1881
and 1885; after Stanton's death, Anthony and then her protégée
Ida Husted Harper continued the project, taking the story up to
1920.

The cost of publication was covered by donations from supporters. Anthony distributed hundreds of the finished volumes
free to colleges and public libraries and to every member of Congress, determined that the heroic history should have a wide
readership. Although the first three volumes cover a range of developments and ideas in the general "advancement" of women
and not just the formal suffrage organizations, it is significant
that Stanton and Anthony called the project the *History of
Woman Suffrage*, demonstrating that for them this had become
the central thread in the struggle for the emancipation of modern
women.

The real effectiveness of the suffrage movement in this period
lay in the persistent and visible activity of a dedicated corps of
leaders who wrote and spoke constantly and kept the movement
in the public eye. There were a number of woman suffrage periodicals, thirty-three in fact between 1870 and 1890, though most
did not last long. The most important was the weekly *Woman's
Journal*, edited by Lucy Stone, then by her daughter Alice Blackwell. The most successful of all the women's rights periodicals, it
ran most of the time in the black and by 1883 was said to have
thirty thousand readers. It acted as a consciousness raiser by col-
lecting every scrap of news on the suffrage front, from abroad as
well as in the United States. At the same time it did not neglect
the wider context of expanding opportunities for women's self-
development. Its regular "What Women Are Doing" column
presented new models of modern womanhood by publicizing

every new breakthrough in educational and work opportunities and celebrating every female "first."

By the 1880s both Stanton and Anthony had become national figures, and women like Livermore and Howe could always command respectful, if unconvinced, audiences. Catcalling and the disruption of meetings were far less frequent than before the Civil War. Even Susan Anthony, plain, angular, and unmarried, the favorite target of the caricaturists' vision of the suffragist as embittered old maid, was now treated with somewhat more respect in the press. Sheer familiarity with her name and photograph was breeding a degree of public tolerance. Like the movement itself, she was becoming a fixture in American life. That, of course, was part of the problem: "The greatest danger threatening our cause, to my mind," wrote the novelist Lillie Devereux Blake, the leader of the New York Suffrage Association, "was that it might drift high and dry into the backwater of respectable indifference—small meetings of nice old ladies in churches, assembling to listen to long-winded arguments on the movement!"

Nevertheless suffrage remained controversial because it would involve women in politics. Most men and women were anxious to maintain the fiction that women were, and should remain, above the inevitably morally tainted realm of party politics. Even suffragists tended to disdain the aggressively masculine world of the parties. "Hordes of men everywhere," sniffed Lillie Devereux Blake, who attended the Republican and Democratic nominating conventions of 1880, "wild, excited masculinity surging through the hotels; . . . the overwhelming odor of tobacco, whisky and boots!"

In fact, women were already involved in political life. Lobbying state or local governments for prohibition or censorship were all political actions, even if prompted by mother love. Women addressing congressional or state legislative committees, women presenting group petitions, women soliciting state appropriations for their charitable work, and women in the anterooms of the halls of power waiting to buttonhole a senator or influential committee chairman were becoming a common sight. Some women even received government patronage. A particularly coveted job was the patronage post of postmistress: by 1893 almost 10 percent of the nation's postmasters were women. As a woman journalist in Washington, D.C., commented as early as 1874, it was no longer a question of "Shall women participate in politics?" but how and on what terms. Scarcely any practicing politicians, however, were ready to make women recognized formal participants in the political process.

If suffragists were having few concrete successes, they could at least congratulate themselves that the women's movement had become international. As the Atlantic crossing became swifter and safer in the 1880s, a growing two-way traffic of speakers and activists developed. Networks of correspondence kept the women's rights press on both sides of the Atlantic up to date on events outside their own country. Out of these contacts came the International Council of Women, which grew into a permanent organization. As the council's founding call declared, it was intended "to impress the important lesson that the position of women anywhere affects their position everywhere." Women were learning to see themselves as part of an international sisterhood, a broad ocean of women, all moving—though at a different pace—toward a world of greater opportunity and influence.

By the mid-1880s, moves to reunite the two suffrage organizations were being urged by the younger members on both sides who did not feel so strongly the bitterness of the original split. The effort was brokered by Lucy Stone's daughter, Alice Blackwell. Anthony and Stone thrashed out the terms of unification and Anthony steered it—or rammed it—through the executive of the NWSA. The new organization would be the National American Woman Suffrage Association (NAWSA), and it would be organized on the AWSA pattern of delegates from state societies, without individual members. At its first meeting in February 1890, Stanton was narrowly elected president and Anthony vice president of the new association.

In 1892 Stanton, now seventy-seven and increasingly disen-
chanted with organizational politics, resigned. She delivered as
her farewell address not a stirring call to further effort but a
meditation on the "Solitude of Self" that has become a modern
feminist classic. It was a call to self-reliance and to courage in the
face of the necessary realization that no one can entirely escape
"the fierce storms of life," and that in the last resort these must be
faced alone. This ultimate solitude, she said, reflected the human
condition of male and female alike, which women could not
evade through male "protection" or vicarious living. The speech
was cheered and widely admired—then as since—but it was out
of line with the direction of the movement, which was toward
solidarity and collective power, and would be increasingly preoc-
cupied with strategic and tactical planning rather than philosophical probing.

Stanton died in 1902 at the age of eighty-seven, rather embittered by feelings that she had been passed over by the younger
generation of suffragists. Anthony took over and ran the
NAWSA until 1900, when at the age of eighty she stepped down.
When she died in 1906, still active in the movement, ten thousand mourners came to pay their respects at her funeral.

The nineteenth century ended with just four suffrage victories
among the states. Wyoming and Utah became states in 1890 and
1896 respectively, with woman suffrage in their constitutions.
Since both had given women the vote as territories, this was not a
very large step forward, but at least it was not a step back. Two
new victories, however—Colorado in 1893 and Idaho in 1896—
gave hope for a winning streak into the twentieth century. The
victory in Colorado was particularly significant because it had
been achieved not by legislative fiat but by a popular male vote in
a referendum, buoyed by the endorsement of the state Populist
movement. In California, however, an eight-month campaign on
a constitutional amendment ended in defeat in 1896, and it
would be another fourteen years before the next victory, even

while American women became more visible in the nation's public life than ever before.

In Massachusetts in 1895 an even more devastating blow had occurred. In an unprecedented though nonbinding referendum, women as well as men had been allowed to express their opinion on extending the vote to women. The result of the referendum showed that men voted against woman suffrage 2 to 1. Women voted overwhelmingly in favor, but of 612,000 women eligible to vote, just over 23,000 actually did so. The male vote was disappointing, but the apparent indifference of most women was deadly. As the only referendum on the vote in which women had actually had the opportunity to take a stand, the Massachusetts results received national publicity and helped to solidify a widely held opinion that most women were either indifferent to or actively opposed to the ballot. Those who wanted it were only a small and odd minority. Such a conclusion was bound to deter the wavering.

But while the great majority of American women might still be voteless, by the 1890s it was no longer possible to ignore women as a factor in the public and economic life of the nation. This was reflected in the arrangements for Chicago's great Columbian Exposition of 1893, a spectacular world's fair celebrating America's material progress that attracted more than 27 million visitors from the United States and abroad. Whereas at the Centennial Exhibition in Philadelphia in 1876 women had been almost entirely ignored by the organizers, this time Congress was prepared to recognize women's contributions to American civilization. It officially appointed a group of Lady Managers, led by Bertha Palmer, wife of a prominent Chicago millionaire, to review all applications for exhibit space from women and women's groups.

The achievements of American women were prominently showcased in a separate and much-visited building designed by Sophia Hayden, a twenty-one-year-old recent graduate of MIT.

The building housed some impressive exhibits, including a collection of four thousand books written by women, and examples
of the inventiveness and productivity of women from ancient
times to the present, from pots and basket weaving to a dish-
washer and new maritime signals in the "Inventions Room."
The building was socially inventive too; besides restaurants and a
model kitchen, run by pioneer home economist Ellen Swallow
Richards, it contained a professionally run day nursery where
women visitors could leave small children while they toured.

While the building triumphantly celebrated "woman" and her
achievements, some potential exhibitors chafed at this group
identification and were affronted at the whole idea of being set
apart as "women" artists or "women" inventors. The painter
Anna Lea Merritt explained that "what we so strongly desire is a
place in the large field," and feared that the "kind ladies who
wish to distinguish us as women would unthinkingly work us
harm." Professional artists who did send their work to the
Woman's Building were rather chagrined at the *inclusiveness* of
the women's art collection, and to find their work shown along-
side "bed quilts, needlework and other rubbish," not to mention
watercolors by Queen Victoria.

Bertha Palmer commissioned her avant-garde friend Mary
Cassatt, an American painter who worked with the Impression-
ist school in France, to do a mural for the building on the subject
of "Modern Woman." Instead of depicting all the various activities that modern American women were undertaking, as had
been expected, Cassatt chose an allegorical approach: a transmut-
ing and transvaluing of the Eve myth. A number of women and
young girls in modern dress were shown picking apples in a
sunny orchard. Here the women joyously plucking fruit from
the Tree of Knowledge and handing it down to their daughters
are ushering in not sin but a new and better world.

A World Congress of Representative Women with delegates
from twenty-seven countries met as part of the fair. Over the
course of a week some 10,000 people listened to 330 papers on

subjects such as the "status of women," "progress of women throughout the world," women's health, the necessity of exercise, and dress reform. Lucy Stone spoke on the "Progress of Fifty Years," emphasizing the advances women had made in education, their improved status in marriage, and the growth of women's organizations. African-American women had no representation on the Board of Lady Managers, but several did address the Congress, among them Frances Watkins Harper, a poet and longtime suffragist and temperance worker, who told a large and appreciative audience what they already knew and delighted to have repeated: "Today we stand on the threshold of woman's era. . . . It is the women of a country who help to mold its character and to influence if not determine its destiny."

The phrase "woman's era" was on everyone's lips. By the turn of the century far less of the world was off limits to women than it had been fifty years earlier. Middle- and upper-class American women at least moved into the twentieth century with a strong sense of possibility, self-confidence, and high self-esteem. While they had not repudiated the home as the center of their sphere, their sense of their own growth out of a life limited to preoccupation with routine housekeeping, fashion, gossip, and personalities carried an implied critique of the old-style domesticity that had molded their former selves. What women looked to as they marched confidently into the next century was a new, improved womanhood and motherhood that would make its decisive imprint on a better society.

# 2

## The New Woman and the New Politics

I wanted all the freedom, all the opportunity, all the equality
there was in the world. I wanted to belong to the human race,
not to a ladies' aid society to the human race.—Rheta Childe
Dorr, *A Woman of Fifty*, 1924

It seems to have been reserved for this generation to work out
new standards of social justice and develop a new basis for our
industrial civilization. Freedom, maternity, education and
morality—all the blessed and abiding interests of childhood and
home are at issue in this supreme struggle.—Margaret Dreier
Robins, 1911

THE NEW WOMAN on her bicycle, pedaling confidently
ahead, might seem a potent symbol of a new age of freedom and
opportunity for women. "It is in the air. It is the woman's era,
and the young women will enter every door that is left ajar," the
lady principal of Grinnell College had confidently proclaimed in
1891. But what women learned in the new century, even while
they continued to make gains, was that access alone did not secure equality or security of participation, and that doors could remain so narrowly ajar that only a few could squeeze through.

Even in education, where the female student might have

seemed well established by 1900, there remained a certain equivocation. The rapid growth in the number of coeds threw some educators into a panic. Many faculty feared that the increasing presence of women was driving out men, not only from the humanities courses but from coeducational institutions altogether. Administrations thus attempted to beef up the proportion of their male students by adding courses in engineering and commerce, and professional schools of law, business, and the like. Most coeducational colleges welcomed the development of the new academic discipline of home economics as a way of steering male and female undergraduates in different directions.

Developed by Ellen Swallow Richards, the first woman to earn a bachelor of science degree from MIT, home economics, or sanitary science as it was often called, at the college level was a serious effort at applied science. Its students were required to study chemistry, biology, and sociology. The aim was not only to apply scientific principles to modernize the administration of the home and family, but also to aid in the "amelioration of the condition of mankind." Graduates were assumed to be involved in the wider affairs of the community. No matter how intellectually serious its aim, however, the field's academic standing suffered from its gender identification. The new home economics departments had an entirely female enrollment and female faculty, while courses in engineering or business, though not officially barred to women, were overwhelmingly male. Still, home economics opened a new career route for many women, who taught the new subject in high schools or colleges, worked on government programs, or even by the 1920s were employed in business.

As old arguments against women's education faded, new ones seemed to emerge. The old tale that college education would make girls into physical and nervous wrecks had been empirically refuted by the increasing number of healthy graduates, but a reworked version resurfaced in the early years of the twentieth century. The census of 1900 revealed an apparent dramatic drop in the birthrate since 1860, particularly among native-born white women. In fact the American birthrate had been dropping steadily since the beginning of the nineteenth century; what made it an issue now was that immigrant women still produced large families, adding to the panic feeling among many "old-stock" Americans of being overrun. The sociologist Edward A. Ross coined the term "race suicide," and President Theodore Roosevelt gave it greater currency when he denounced the marriage-and-motherhood-avoiding woman as comparable to the soldier who shirks his duty.

The decline in the birthrate was most evident among the professional classes, and most commentators turned the spotlight on the highly educated woman. Diverted by "male" studies in college, seduced by the allure of a career and financial independence, she was seen to be rejecting her natural destiny. Numerous surveys showed that the female college graduate was indeed less likely to marry than the average woman. By the second decade of the twentieth century, as more young women attended college, their marriage rate approached the norm. But a striking 50 percent of the female college graduates of the 1880s and '90s remained unmarried.

If four years of college were a time of preparation for a young man's adult life, it was still not at all clear to most female students where these years should lead for them. Most of the women who graduated by 1912 did not become "career women," but more than 60 percent held jobs at some point in their lives, and those who did not often felt a vague guilt for not making better use of their education.

Next only to education, work had held a special place in the ideology and psychology of the broad women's movement from its beginning. As they contemplated the lives of their female contemporaries, it seemed to women activists that womanhood was divided into two unequal parts: the majority were condemned to a soul-deadening drudgery, either in the home or in the exploitative jobs available to women, while a minority lived as petted "butterflies" sheltered from all responsibility and important work.

Even most middle-class married women were hardly idle, but their daughters were becoming acutely aware by the end of the century that the nonwage-earning middle-class daughter or wife was an expensive item to maintain. Indeed, attempts to explain the late marriage ages of professional men often pointed to the expense of singlehandedly maintaining a family in the urban upper-middle-class world. It was hard for urban daughters to feel that the odd tasks they performed around the house "helping mother," or the conventional round of socializing, was necessary or a just return for the expense of their upkeep. Work came to have a meaning for many of them beyond the personal independence that a salary could bring: it was justification for their education, indeed for their existence, and it linked them to the wider exciting world of endeavor and achievement. In any case, the continuing uncertainties of a vibrant but unstable economy meant that many middle-class women could not live in the prescribed fashion, protected by and dependent on a man, as husbands and fathers died or lost their money. "You ought to look squarely in the face," wrote Congressman William Breckinridge of Kentucky, encumbered with a large family, to his daughter Sophonisba, "that if I die, you will have to make your own living: & if I live you may have to do so anyhow."

That a young woman should be trained to be self-supporting and not passively accept marriage as her only option in life was a message that women's rights advocates had been delivering for years. The suffragist Mary Livermore had made it the center of her highly successful and oft-repeated public lecture of the 1880s, "What Shall We Do with Our Daughters?," indicating that the answer could no longer automatically be to "marry them off as soon as possible." Training for a "trade, paying business, or a profession," Livermore urged, even if she used it only intermittently, would give a woman security and self-confidence, and save her from that "vague terror" with which "aimless untrained women" regarded the future.

The prospects for worthwhile and remunerative work for women had seemed encouraging at the turn of the century. *What Can a Woman Do?* was the title of a popular 1893 book, whose author discussed as realistic options journalism, law, medicine, government clerkships, business, "stenography and typewriting" telegraphy, and work as a saleswoman. Books and magazines were filled with advice on, as one title had it, *How to Make Money Although a Woman* (1895). The young graduate would find many older women pointing out how numerous the opportunities were compared to when they were young. Lucy Stone recalled that when she was a girl, "I seemed to be shut out of everything I wanted to do"; the only jobs open to women were teaching, dressmaking, some factory work, and domestic service. But now, she exulted, when her daughter Alice graduated from Boston University in 1881 "she might do what she chose; all the professions were open to her; she could enter any line of business."

Yet while the *Woman's Journal* constantly ran articles on the "first" women to take up new kinds of work or enter the professions, these pioneers were seldom followed by large numbers of other women. It may be significant that Alice Stone Blackwell did *not* venture into any of the professions or business; she worked with her parents in the women's suffrage movement and helped edit its journal. That is, she did what many women graduates did: she worked in a woman's milieu, even if a newly created one. The pattern that was developing in the field of education replicated itself in the professions and the world of white-collar work. Once women were in, they were either shunted or voluntarily moved toward separate specialties while men fell back and regrouped around an inner bastion that was more secure against female pressure.

By the early twentieth century women were certainly represented in the professions, though in the major "male" professions of medicine, law, and higher education their position remained marginal. Still, by 1900 there were almost nine thousand women physicians, including more than a hundred African-American women; 10 percent of medical students were women and, by 1910, 6 percent of medical practitioners. "Medical women," proclaimed a woman physician triumphantly in 1900, "are now accepted as a fact of civilization."

After 1910, however, the proportion of women in medicine began to decline, and did not reach the 1910 figure of 6 percent again until the early 1960s. At the beginning of the century a vigorous campaign by the American Medical Association to upgrade standards of medical education resulted in the closing of many medical schools, including most of those specifically for women. Wary of being "overwhelmed" by female applicants, many of the remaining "male" schools limited the number of female applicants they would accept. In 1917 the dean of Johns Hopkins defended coeducation in medical school but advised that the proportion of women should never exceed 25 percent. Above that liminal point "the school would gradually become feminized and men would desert it in favor of others in which there were fewer or no women." Twenty-five percent was generous; most medical schools imposed a quota of around 5 percent. And as doctors increasingly gained control of hospitals, fewer were willing to admit women to internships. At the same time it seems that many women seeking useful and interesting professional work who in the past might have tried to pursue a medical career were now choosing the newly developing "helping profession" of social work, which was more open to women.

The law was a harder nut to crack than medicine, and attracted fewer women. Even though the first woman had been called to the bar in 1872, by 1910 there were still only fifteen hundred women lawyers in the United States, and most of these worked in government, edited legal journals, or worked in their husbands' offices, often doing work that would nowadays be done by secretaries or paralegals. By 1930 women still made up

only 2 percent of American lawyers, though many women found
their legal training useful in reform and feminist work, even if
they did not practice law.

The churches were the most difficult arena of all for women.
Unitarians and Congregationalists ordained the occasional
woman, but the Catholic church, Episcopalians, Methodists, and
Baptists (the latter two being the largest Protestant denomina-
tions) all remained adamant against the ordination of women, as
did Judaism, even though the Reform movement had broken
down many Orthodox Jewish customs.

The major employers of academic women were the women's
colleges. In the coeducational colleges, women were usually to be
found as either deans of women, a largely administrative post, or
in women's specialties such as home economics or social work.
Women had established themselves in social work from its beginnings, and it remained one of the most hospitable fields to
women and women's leadership. Home economics departments
were often refuges for women chemists in the absence of many
other options. By later standards, college women in the late nineteenth century were remarkably interested in science and mathe-
matics, and by 1910 there were 204 women's names in a
Directory of American Scientists. But the emerging culture of
laboratory research science, which saw it as hard, objective, impersonal, and male, militated against opening scarce research positions to women, as did the assumption that at least some would
marry and thus their training would be wasted. A few outstanding women scientists, such as the medical researcher Florence
Sabin at Johns Hopkins, won prestigious positions. Despite her
successful career there, however, even she found that she could
not be appointed head of her department.

The emerging pattern for women in science was acceptance of
the occasional "star" and the routing of other women either into
teaching at women's colleges—where much of their time would
be taken up with undergraduate instruction, and where they
would miss informal interaction with the best male scientists in

their field—or into women's specialties such as home economics. Most women who remained in the male scientific mainstream operated at an ancillary level as lab and research assistants, unless, like Alice Hamilton, a toxicologist, they could move into a field that interested few men. Hamilton practically invented a new specialty of industrial medicine through research on lead poisoning and the linking of disease to environmental causes. She noted that her male medical friends had little interest in these topics, nor did the major American medical journals and textbooks. "I gained the impression," she noted dryly, "that here was a subject tainted with Socialism or with feminine sentimentality for the poor."

This pattern had been anticipated as early as 1870 by John Raymond, the first president of Vassar College. Raymond thought that women had a special role to play in "scientific investigation," particularly in tasks requiring patience and delicate manipulation—the kind of work that young men could not do so well and "would not want to if they could." Reminding his audience that Eve had been created as a helpmeet for a man, he insisted that whenever women and men worked together, "the former is naturally subsidiary and auxiliary to the latter." Women, he thought, were unlikely to make any great original breakthroughs in science, "but as associates and aids they are admirable." This might stand for the entire pattern of women's work as it evolved for the next hundred years.

Even when women established themselves in a profession, they had to cope with the uneasy knowledge that they were foreigners in alien territory, working amid a general assumption that they would not make the grade. One strategy was to make themselves as inconspicuous as possible and avoid situations where they might be humiliated by rejection. The early women interns at Johns Hopkins spent their rest periods in the nurses' sitting room rather than the doctor's lounge because, as one recalled many years later, "46 years ago we still felt on sufferance and wished to be unobtrusive." At Berkeley in the first decade of the century, the only two women faculty members never attended faculty meetings—"it would have prejudiced the men against us." Women agonized over whether they should attend the social events of their professional associations or whether it would be more tactful to stay away and thus not embarrass the men or put a damper on male sociability. Designating a social event a "smoker" was a message in clear code to women that it was intended to be for men only.

Part of the problem, in this period of rapid change at the turn of the century, was still, as one Bryn Mawr undergraduate had pointed out in 1888, a "lack of theoretical conclusions as to what the idea of a woman's life should be." To a great many people the whole idea of a professional woman was anomalous. Mary Putnam Jacobi, who became a distinguished doctor, complained that people always seemed to judge a woman professional by extraprofessional criteria. The basic question men asked of a woman doctor was not "Is she capable? but 'Is this fearfully capable person nice?' Will she upset our ideal of womanhood, . . . and the social relation of the sexes? Can a woman physician be lovable; can she marry; can she have children; will she take care of them? If she cannot, what is she?"

How were men to regard and deal with these new female additions to their world? Could a woman be a colleague in the same way as a man? The entrance of women meant rethinking the nature of the professions: Were they essentially genderless activities in which the sex of the worker was immaterial, or were they specifically masculine endeavors which the entrance of women would, or should, transform? Most male professionals were not only irritated by the "intrusion" of women into their world, they were reluctant to think of their own sex as irrelevant to their occupation. Male lawyers emphasized the adversarial nature of courtroom work, which required virile nerves. Professional work, most men insisted, required the capacity for objectivity—a strictly gendered quality. The more intellectual the work, the more it seems men were anxious to see the capacity to fearlessly face "cold, hard facts," without flinching or personal bias, as requiring a positively soldierly fortitude that only men possessed.

Women too were confused over the relation of gender and professionalism. Those who were thoroughly imbued with a belief in a distinctive and morally superior female nature thought that the professions would be improved by the infusion of a feminine perspective and womanly virtues. Others insisted that gender should be irrelevant to professional conduct. "Be *lawyers*," one woman advised her colleagues bluntly, "don't be lady lawyers." As late as 1910 the journalist Margaret Deland was still irritated by the Woman's Building at the 1893 Columbian Exposition, which she considered to have been "a mortifying and humiliating display. . . . Such insistence upon sex in work is an insult to the work, and to the sex, too."

Two pioneer women physicians, Elizabeth Blackwell and Mary Putnam Jacobi, had sharply different perspectives on the relation of gender to professional medicine. Blackwell, born in 1821 and the first American woman to earn a medical degree, approached medicine as a moral enterprise in great need of women's "spiritual power of maternity." She saw health as a holistic package of the physical and the spiritual, maintained by living according to natural laws; it was the physician's task to guide the patient to live by these laws. This was a perspective that led her to reject such modern developments as bacteriology, vivisection, and most gynecological surgery. Jacobi, on the other hand, who was some twenty years younger, had come to medicine out of a passionate interest in science. She felt that Blackwell had never really been interested in medicine as such, and that this hampered her capacity as a physician. While Blackwell told women students always to bear in mind the power and responsibility they had as women physicians, Jacobi told them to remember "that you are, first of all, physicians."

Larger issues were neatly encapsulated in anxieties about how professional women should dress. Women's clothing had long

been a subject of amusement as impractical and foolishly extrav-
agant; cartoons ridiculing women doctors often showed a female
surgeon, scalpel in hand, dressed in a fussy, beribboned frock. At
the other extreme, the notorious Dr. Mary Walker had adopted
male clothing in the 1860s and caused a scandal by doing so. The
most widely adopted solution in the 1890s was the shirtwaist plus
a tailored jacket with broad shoulders. Dr. Josephine Baker, the
first woman executive in the New York City Department of
Health, gratefully adopted this costume because it meant that
"when a masculine colleague of mine looked around the office in
a rather critical state of mind, no feminine furbelows would
catch his eye and give him an excuse to become irritated by the
presence of a woman where according to him, no woman had a
right to be." Mary Walker, Dr. Baker pointed out, had worn
"trousers to startle men into recognizing that a woman was demanding man's rights. I wore a standard costume—almost a uniform—because the last thing I wanted was to be conspicuously
feminine when working with men."

Inconspicuousness and not challenging norms of womanliness
were one way to fit in. Indeed, as an attribute inconspicuousness
could be *demanded* of the woman professional. Harvard University eventually offered Alice Hamilton an assistant professorship
in 1919, but only on condition that she never use the faculty club
nor embarrass the faculty by marching in the commencement
procession and sitting on the platform.

While they hovered on the margins of the major professions,
women did become firmly ensconced in the "semi-professions"
of teaching, nursing, and librarianship. Since these were less
prestigious, less well paid, and offered less autonomy, they were
far more open to women. So much so, indeed, that they soon became entirely or predominantly female occupations—which ensured that they would remain of lower prestige and lower pay.
By 1890, 65 percent of schoolteachers were women, and by 1910,
77 percent. Turnover was high, and women earned about 60 percent of the male salary in 1890, less than half by 1910. Because

most black children went to segregated schools, teaching was one of the few white-collar jobs open to African-American women. The great expansion in the number of public libraries at the turn of the century opened new positions for genteel, educated, but cheap labor, and by 1910 women made up 79 percent of all American librarians. Women did not drive men out of these professions entirely; rather they drove them *up*. Men remained the librarians of prestigious university libraries, and they became the head librarians in the public system; in teaching, men kept the jobs in boys' private schools, and in the public system they were more likely than women to teach the higher grades and to be principals and administrators.

The first training schools for nurses were established in the 1870s; ultimately they transformed nursing from something that all women were supposed to be able to do from instinct into a profession. In 1900 there were 11,804 graduate nurses, and by 1920 more than 149,000. Nursing was an entirely female profession, and the medical field developed into a classic two-tier system with all doctors (over 90 percent male), however junior, superior to all nurses (100 percent female), however senior. At the same time nursing presented new economic opportunities to middle- and lower-middle-class young women, and the nurses' separate world offered its own opportunities for promotion, prestige, and responsibility, without the need to compete with men.

The business world of the early twentieth century was increasingly dominated by large-scale corporate organization, where women were welcome only at the lower levels. But there was still room for the smaller-scale individual entrepreneur who might sometimes be a woman. Independent businesswomen were most likely to be successful if they could exploit a niche market catering specifically to other women, like the developing beauty business. Madame C. J. Walker, the child of ex-slaves, became a self-made millionaire by developing new hair products directed at the African-American market, and in the process

opened up new "pink-collar" jobs for black women. Katherine
Gibbs saw the business potential of thousands of young women
who wanted to learn how to use the new typewriter, and opened
a chain of schools to teach them. Candace Wheeler invented the
new business of interior decorating, where there were no established male practitioners. Where there was no gender or race
niche to be filled, the support of influential patrons could be crucial. Julia Morgan, the first woman to graduate from the College
of Engineering at Berkeley in 1894, achieved considerable success as an independent architect aided by the patronage of the
wealthy Phoebe Hearst and then her son William Randolph
Hearst, as well as by a community of organized activist women
who gave her commissions to design YWCA buildings and
women's clubhouses.

Below the professional and entrepreneurial level, striking
changes occurred in the kinds of wage work available to women.
In 1870 half of all women wage earners worked as domestic servants; by 1920 only one-sixth did so. Women deserted domestic
service as soon as new opportunities arose. Industry did not necessarily offer higher wages and almost always provided harsher
working conditions, but it did offer freedom from being always
on call, and it offered a kind of equality. The working girl might
have a boss, but she did not have a mistress.

While the largely immigrant girls and women working in factories or urban sweatshops invoked increasing social concern, the
phenomenon that struck contemporary observers most forcibly
was the growing number of young women working in offices,
manipulating typewriters. The great expansion in the scale of
business after the Civil War and the growth of the federal bureaucracy as well as the bureaucratic organization of corporations offered new opportunities to young women. Business needs
coincided with the increasing availability of young women with
some high school education whose labor was no longer absorbed
by the farm and who could be employed at lower wages than
men. By the 1880s young women were flocking to the cities from

farms and small towns, seeking job opportunities apart from teaching, and a better and more interesting life than they perceived their mothers as having. More and more of them found those opportunities in the office.

Whereas a mere 2 percent of office workers had been women in 1870, by 1920 they were 45 percent, and 92 percent of stenographers. The rapid expansion transformed what had been the male space of the business office into a workplace where both sexes mingled, though seldom on quite the same level. Young women hired for office work were invariably referred to as "business girls," but as the routinization and subdivision of office work progressed, it became clear that they were in no sense the female equivalent of the "businessman." The woman's sector of the business world came to consist of a pool of mostly young women doing fairly routine work, with rapid turnover, and a very short and specialized ladder of advancement. Fewer male clerks than in the past had the possibility of advancing into management; women in the office had none. But as a workplace the office was generally healthy, the hours reasonable, the pay good compared to most other kinds of women's work. Like the college experience of more academic young women, the office was often an interesting and enjoyable interlude between childhood and the adult destiny of marriage and motherhood, in which the young woman made friends, had a good time, and quite often met the man she would marry.

The world of clerical work was overwhelmingly white and largely native-born; so was the new world of women sales clerks in department stores. Saleswomen worked very long hours and were not well paid, but sales was regarded, like office work, as a genteel and respectable kind of employment, considerably above factory work. And for the ambitious woman there was always the possibility of promotion to buyer—an interesting and well-paid position. By 1920 almost half of department store buyers were women.

Business adaptations of new technology that had not been im-

mediately appropriated by men opened up other new employment opportunities for women. In the 1880s the new telephone
companies began to hire women exclusively as telephone opera-
tors, and by the early twentieth century Bell Telephone was the
largest single employer of women in the United States. By 1900,
13 percent of professional photographers were women, and
many more worked as assistants in studios, developing and re-
touching prints. Neither department stores nor telephone companies would employ African-American women, however, and
only black-owned businesses employed them for office work.

While the numbers of women working in factories and sweatshops also increased, it was the female white-collar workers that
observers saw as indices of basic changes in women's lives and in
social organization. As one commentator remarked in 1913, to
stand in the station of a large city in the early morning and "ob-
serve the thousands of young work-women who arrive on every
incoming train" was to be struck by "the fact that much of the
work of that great city is in the hands of these competent-looking
young girls." These were women who lived a significant part of
their day outside a family and domestic setting, and they were
forcing many men for the first time to interact with women on a
level that was neither social nor domestic. The journalist Rheta
Dorr in 1910 saw it as highly significant that "nine million
women" in paid labor outside the home were "rapidly passing
from the domestic control of their fathers and husbands."

Most middle-class working girls continued to live at home,
but a growing number, along with the new professional women,
were making the experiment of living independently in the city.
This development was both intriguing and alarming. Magazine
articles and government reports spoke of "women adrift" and
worried about the young women's vulnerability to sexual predators. But a more admiring epithet that quickly came into use was
"bachelor girl" or "bachelor woman." The female bachelor was
something quite different from the "spinster" or the "old maid":
the latter always bore the connotations of pathos, of faded left-

behindness, but the bachelor girl took on some of the aura of the male bachelor—freedom and boldness. A visiting Frenchwoman in a restaurant marveled: "I saw the girls known as 'bachelor girls' call for the bill of fare as naturally as if they were bachelors indeed."

Other commentators were far more ambivalent about the bachelor girl. The psychologist G. Stanley Hall, a pioneer in the new study of adolescence, denounced her as an evolutionary dead end, unlikely ever to settle down, marry, or have children. What is interesting about Hall, however, is not his denunciation but his reluctant attraction. "These women," he wrote, "are very attractive as companions . . . their very look, step, and bearing is free; . . . they are at home with the racket and on the golf links; they are splendid friends; their minds . . . are as attractive as their bodies. . . . These women are often in every way magnificent, only they are not mothers. . . ."

By the turn of the century, wage work was becoming part of the general experience of a larger proportion of the American female population. By the twenties half of all adult American women had worked outside the home at some point in their lives. At the same time, for most women, this experience was short-lived. Native-born white women in clerical occupations tended to work between the ages of eighteen and twenty-four, between leaving high school and getting married; immigrant women in industry started earlier, as young as fourteen, and left to marry earlier. For both groups, workforce participation after marriage was generally episodic, since the general expectation among both men and women was that wives were supported by husbands and would not take outside employment. Not until the census of 1910 were enumerators even told specifically to ask married women to state their occupations. This new pattern in women's lives thus meant a much sharper break than ever before between the world of young womanhood, much of which was now extrafamilial, and the world of domesticity they entered on marriage.

Central to that domesticity was motherhood, and the concept of motherhood played a key and often contradictory role in the continuing debate over the role of women in the early twentieth century. Actual or potential motherhood came to shape women's legal rights and their claim on the state. As the birthrate fell and the use of contraception spread, the apparent "rejection" of motherhood became a symbol of the socially deplorable consequences of woman's emancipation. On the other hand, women were beginning to conceive of motherhood in a particularly expansive way, which justified their growing involvement in public life. The problems of poor women as both mothers and workers were at the core of the activities of the "women's social justice wing" of the larger progressive movement for reform that swept through the United States from the 1890s to World War I.

It was clear by the 1890s that the worst effects of the industrialism that had transformed American life, operating with little government regulation, needed mitigating. City government needed to be made more efficient and more honest; giant corporations and their wealth needed to be reined in. Political, social, and legal thinkers were promoting the concept of the "public good" as a necessary corrective to the automatic privileging of individual property and contract rights.

Women were a vital part of this tide of progressive reform, both as activists and as beneficiaries. Women, and children too, seemed to suffer most from the exploitative aspects of the modern economy. As workers they were the worst paid and least able to control their work conditions; as mothers they had to cope with the problems of urban slums and caring for their children with inadequate resources. By the early twentieth century significant numbers of organized and educated women were constituting themselves as champions of the more downtrodden and helpless of their sex, and in the process playing a significant public role in the creation of the modern welfare state.

The advance guard of the women's wing of progressive reform was the settlement house. Settlements drew the recent college graduate to active engagement with the problems she had studied in her college classes and thus to useful involvement in the social question. One of the first, and always the most famous, of these settlements was Hull House in Chicago, founded in 1891 by the twenty-nine-year-old Jane Addams, the restless daughter of an Illinois state senator. In only a few years Hull House burgeoned into a hub of activity. By 1895 it had twenty residents, almost all of them young college-educated women, linked to a larger group of volunteers. The Hull House community offered to the polyglot peoples of the neighborhood an array of services from English classes to various kinds of adult education, and acted as ombudsman for the local people in dealing with city authorities.

Addams publicized the settlement idea through her speeches and writings, and by 1900 there were a hundred settlements in American cities, often sustained by the donations of wealthy patrons and by successful fund-raising among the socially aware of the upper class, especially women. Hull House, for example, depended a great deal on the support of the exclusive Chicago Woman's Club, of which Jane Addams was a member. Over the years the settlements built a network of alliances with women's clubs and organizations, and with sympathetic and reform-minded men who could assist them in their increasingly ambitious projects. Hull House, in particular, had close relations with the sociology and philosophy departments at the University of Chicago, and men like John Dewey and the sociologist W. I. Thomas were frequent visitors.

By the mid-1890s, after the terrible depression and winter of 1893, Hull House and other settlements moved from the role of "facilitators" and educators for their communities toward active reform efforts. The women of the settlements, along with other educated women who worked for the growing number of reform organizations and social agencies, were carving out new careers for themselves as professional social workers, investigators, and reformers. Several universities began to offer formal training in social work, and by 1910 the majority of settlement residents were working as salaried government inspectors, lecturers in social work, or workers in juvenile protective agencies. It was largely they who investigated the working and living conditions of the urban poor, who compiled statistics, who helped to draft legislation that male politicians and lawyers could put into action. They were backed by the growing army of "organized womanhood" in the club movement who, swayed by the changing political climate of the times, were turning their attention to problems of social reform, especially those concerning women and children.

Once turned in this direction, clubwomen became a powerful constituency for reform activists. "The spectacle of 275,000 women splendidly organized, armed with leisure and opportunity, and animated by a passion for reform assumes the distinction of a 'social force,'" noted the *Atlantic Monthly* in 1904. Clubwomen not only embarked on numerous local campaigns for better schools, more efficient garbage collection, and purer milk supplies but were also important supporters of the federal Pure Food and Drug Act of 1906 and crucial allies in major campaigns for the protection of women as laborers and as mothers.

Of particular importance was the National Congress of Mothers, organized in 1897, which by 1910 had fifty thousand members. They were a powerful lobby for the right of mothers to the legal guardianship of their children, for compulsory school attendance laws and the restriction of child labor, and for the creation of a separate juvenile justice system that would be remedial rather than punitive. The members were inspired by a belief in the natural nurturing qualities given women by their reproductive potential; but they were also affected by the new outlook that instinct alone was not enough. Many were particularly concerned about the inadequacies of poor and immigrant mothers and the problems of their children, especially when the mothers worked outside the home. What the world needed was better motherhood; thus they lobbied for domestic science and child-study classes in schools. Twentieth-century mothers needed to be prepared for their job by education and developed expertise.

"We are stateswomen," declared one speaker proudly to the Congress of Mothers, yet women justified their new activism in civic affairs not so much by reformulating their own role as by reconceiving the nature of the state itself. Frances Willard had once said that her ambition was to make the world so homelike that women could freely go out into it everywhere. Other activist women used the language of the family to express a new conception of the state. When women had the vote, predicted Rheta Dorr, the nation would become "like a great, well-ordered, comfortable sanitary household. . . . Everyone, as in a family, will have enough to eat. . . . All the family will be taken care of."

To reconceive the state as a home implied broadening the concept of justice away from a narrow concentration on individual rights to incorporate an ethic of care based on concern for the most vulnerable. The activist Abby Morton Diaz, speaking of her own organization that aimed to bring women together across class boundaries, explained, "I do not mean by this that equality is possible. It is not found even in families. Kinship is." The middle-class reforming clubwoman thus came to regard the working girls and women for whom she felt a new responsibility not as aliens, nor quite as equal fellow citizens, but rather as poor relations who had a natural claim to be protected both from outside exploitation and quite often from their own feckless habits.

To see the state as a home was implicitly—and automatically—to give mothers a larger role as its chief executive. This expansive view of motherhood had two advantages. Traditionally motherhood had been cited as a major reason why women could not participate in public life, because of the time and concentration needed for the care of children and because the emotional qualities desirable for mothering would be counterproductive outside the home. Now women were insisting that it was motherhood that made women's activity in the public sphere necessary, and indeed a duty, to protect not only their own children but all children, and even other women. Moreover, the motherly qualities of sympathy and nurture were assumed to be natural to all women, whether or not they had actually given birth, and when combined with modern education and expertise they gave single women the authority to assume a public role on behalf of children's welfare.

One place they conspicuously did so was in the Children's Bureau, first proposed in 1906 and created in 1912 under the persistent prodding of settlement women like Jane Addams and Lillian Wald as a federal government research and advocacy agency for the welfare of children. The Children's Bureau had a small budget and was staffed entirely by single women, headed by Julia Lathrop of Hull House. The bureau retained close ties with the settlement houses and other women's reform groups, and provided a small but well-connected group of professional women with a tiny beachhead in the federal government. Lathrop and her colleagues concentrated on the promotion of child health and efforts to curb the extremely high rate of infant mortality in the United States. This could be traced to many causes, economic and environmental, but the Children's Bureau women concentrated on an area that seemed more safely within their purview and that they could do something concrete to rectify: maternal ignorance. One of their most successful projects was the publication of two free booklets, *Infant Care* and *Prenatal Care*. The thousands of letters they received from poor women asking for advice was an indication not only of a mobile modern world in which the writers' own mothers might well be across the continent or across the ocean, but also that the writers themselves no longer found the traditional handed-down wisdom to be sufficiently modern and scientific.

While traditional mothering came to seem inadequate and in need of sound advice, social and professional mothering was a powerful vehicle to increase women's involvement in the public world and give them a claim on public power. It was becoming clear that the male trade-union movement, dominated by the skilled men of the American Federation of Labor, had little interest in organizing women workers. Nor did working women, most of whom were young, unskilled, and transitory, generally have the capacity to organize effective unions or otherwise protect themselves against appalling work conditions and exploitative employers. Middle- and upper-class women began to take on the role of protector of working women and girls.

One influential upper-middle-class organization formed for this purpose was the National Consumers' League, founded in 1898 with the aim of forcing factory and store owners to improve working conditions by bringing to bear the moral and economic power of women as consumers. The morally conscientious consumer, the League advised, should be aware of the conditions in which the goods she bought were produced, and patronize only those establishments that received a "white label" from League investigators. Under its dynamic general secretary Florence Kelley, the League became a powerful force in the general reform coalition.

Cross-class sympathy was taken even further by the Women's Trade Union League (WTUL), founded in 1903 in New York City by a small group of working women in alliance with some middle- and upper-class women reformers. By 1915 the WTUL had become national with branches in twenty-two cities, most importantly in New York and Chicago. It was based on the premise that a cross-class organization of women was possible, and that the role of the privileged "allies," as they called themselves, should be not to direct but to empower the working-class members and help them develop their own capacities. The WTUL also had a significant women's rights edge since the upper-middle-class leaders were already committed to women's suffrage, and they converted the talented young labor activists like Rose Schneiderman, whom they groomed for leadership. They in turn helped link the suffrage movement and working women.

In spite of much goodwill and a genuine commitment to the

labor movement by the middle- and upper-class allies, however, there were continuing tensions in this cross-class alliance. Just as working-class girls felt intimidated in male union meetings, they also felt intimidated by the often college-educated allies, who were usually some ten years older, Protestant, and native-born, unlike the largely immigrant Jewish and Catholic workers. Margaret Dreier, president of the WTUL, was an extremely wealthy woman and for much of the time kept the organization going largely from her own pocket—which also retarded the emergence of working women into leadership positions. Still, the WTUL nurtured the talents of outstanding young labor leaders like Pauline Newman, Rose Schneiderman, and Mary Anderson.

Initially the working girls were romanticized by middle-class activists. The New York suffragist Henrietta Rodman rhapsodized: "Our sisters of the poorer class have the most fundamental right for which we are struggling—the right for economic independence." Closer contact, however, often brought disillusionment. As part of the muckraking and exposé culture of the period, a number of middle-class women took a factory or shop job for a while as a means of both sharing and discovering the "real" world of the working-class girl. Such excursions, like Dorothy Richardson's 1905 *The Long Day* (1905) and Mrs. John Van Vorst and Marie Van Vorst's *The Woman Who Toils: Being the Experience of Two Ladies as Factory Girls* (1903)—its very title sums up the importance of class—often left the middle-class visitor properly outraged at the long hours and terrible working conditions, but also irritated at what she considered the sloppy work habits of the workers, their frivolous conversations and absorption in romance, and the way they wasted their money on unsuitable and tawdry fashions.

Most disillusioning for the middle-class allies was the workers' lack of commitment to work, to improving their skills, and so therefore also to union organization. For the allies, work was emancipation and identity; it freed them from the traditional fate of having to marry for a living, and it was a matter of self-respect. They could not see that for the working girl, only marriage would free her from the grind of the factory or shop and, above all, from the constrictions of the parental home. No doubt the girls were oversanguine in assuming marriage would mean they would never have to "work" again, or that the drudgery of home and children in the domestic setting affordable by most working-class men would be any less than that in the factory. Nevertheless marriage would give them a home of their own and status in their community. Realistically, for most working-class women, secure access to a male wage through marriage was a better bet for improving their condition than a lifetime commitment to factory or workshop labor outside the home.

Despite their tendency to look upon work as temporary, the potential for militancy among young working girls was demonstrated forcibly in the great 1909 ILGWU strike of some twenty thousand shirtwaist workers in New York City—85 percent of them women. The 1909 strike was the largest ever in a woman-dominated industry and the first in a series of mass strikes in the early 1910s of mainly female workers in the Northeast and Midwest garment industry. The numbers and the gender composition of strikers and picketers struck the public imagination and brought considerable and generally sympathetic press coverage, especially when middle-class supporters of the WTUL joined the picketers and a number of wealthy women publicly demonstrated their support.

Middle-class observers, however, were often disconcerted by the appearance of the strikers. A woman reporter for *Collier's* magazine remarked on the strikers' elaborate hairstyles, shirtwaists, and large hats. She had expected a strike to be "somber," with mothers "wiping their eyes with their aprons," but had found a scene of "gaiety and flirtation." The girls did not look "as if they had any grievance." Other newspapers noted that the strikers looked "prosperous" and "well dressed" and certainly "looked far from starving or downtrodden." By the 1890s not only were many articles of women's dress available ready-made, but cheap knockoffs of uptown fashions were quickly available at prices that working girls could just stretch their budgets to afford. Large hats that could be extravagantly decorated tended to be the first purchase "of their own" by young immigrant women—their assertion of equality with the native-born. Perched on top of hair piled high on the head, the extremely large hats of the period virtually forced the wearer to hold her head up and look straight ahead. When the immigrant girl exchanged the head shawl for the American hat, it was not just a gesture of assimilation but a new and bolder style of self-presentation.

For a middle-class public to sympathize with women strikers, it was apparently necessary for them to be obvious objects of pity; but the workers did not perceive themselves in this way, and they wished to present themselves at their best—as "ladies" with just demands for consideration and respect in the workplace, not just for a living wage but for a decent life. The young strike leader Clara Lemlich defiantly defended the strikers' "finery": "We're human, all of us girls, and we're young. We like new hats as well as any other young woman. Why shouldn't we?"

The strike eventually ended on less than satisfactory terms for the workers, and two years later in 1911 New York was appalled by the terrible fire at the Triangle shirtwaist factory in which 146 young women were killed. In spite of the militancy and the publicity given to the garment workers, by 1913 still only 6 percent of women workers were organized in unions, and by 1912 both the working women and their allies in the WTUL were turning toward protective legislation to mitigate the hardship of working women's lives. Like other women in reform circles, the WTUL leaders had concluded that women did not in the long run have the strength to defend themselves, nor sufficient clout to defend others without the powerful aid of the state.

Protective legislation would become the major means of dealing with the problems of working women, and a key figure in the effort to achieve it was Florence Kelley. Kelley, the daughter of a Pennsylvania congressman, had taken a Ph.D. in Zurich, married a Polish radical, become a socialist, borne three children, divorced her abusive husband, and in 1891 at age thirty-two turned up on the doorstep of Hull House, looking for refuge. She was a committed radical, a correspondent and translator of Friedrich Engels, a suffragist and member of the NAWSA, and a dynamo. From her base in the Consumers' League she agitated tirelessly for the protection of women workers and for the elimination of child labor.

Ideally Kelley would have liked to see legislated protection for all workers. What could be achieved in this regard, however, was constrained by the opposition of business groups, the preference of the AFL's skilled male unions to negotiate independently with employers rather than be restricted by legislation, and, above all, by the attitude of the courts. Dedicated to the sanctity of private property and contracts, including the right of the worker to "freely contract" with an employer for terms, the courts had made it clear by the twentieth century that they would very narrowly scrutinize any "welfare" legislation. Laws restricting hours or laying down a minimum for wages had been struck down by the courts when they were written in gender-neutral language and thus applied also to men. But the courts did accept the "police power" of the state to override contract rights when the general health and welfare was at stake, and they had shown some willingness to consider women, like children, subject to different rules than men.

This was a loophole that women reformers could exploit. When the Oregon courts struck down legislation restricting the hours of women factory and laundry workers, Florence Kelley and other women reformers determined to make this a test case before the U.S. Supreme Court. They secured the services of the lawyer Louis Brandeis, whose sister-in-law Josephine Goldmark, a member of the National Consumers' League, and others wrote the famous "Brandeis Brief" for the 1907 case, based on extensive research in American and European investigations into the effects of overlong hours on women's health. One of their major points—and this was the point taken up by the Court—was that long hours destroyed a woman's health and thus impaired her future capacity as a mother as well as her ability to perform adequately her duties in the family.

Justice David Brewer, speaking for the Court in upholding the protective legislation, rested his decision mainly on the proposition that women were not primarily workers in the same way that men were. Nor, in spite of considerable changes in her situation, was a woman in any real sense "an equal competitor with her brother." Women, because they were women, would always be "where some legislation to protect her seems necessary to secure a real equality of right ... her physical structure and a proper discharge of her maternal functions—having in view not merely her own health, but the well being of the race—justify legislation to protect her from the greed as well as the passion of man." A legislated reduction in hours, though it restricted her rights of contract, was for her own good and for the good of society as a whole, which had an interest in preserving the health of the mothers and potential mothers of future citizens.

Thus the Court insisted that woman's capacity for motherhood was more important to society than her contributions as a worker. At the same time Brewer made a point that Kelley herself found increasingly compelling—that it was unjust and injurious to impose a formal equality where no substantive equality in fact existed—and, Brewer implied, never would. Women needed the protection of the state in a way that men did not, and the state in turn had a right to protect its own interest in their reproductive capacity.

*Muller v. Oregon* opened the way for further efforts in protection, and by 1914 twenty-seven states had legislation restricting the hours that women might work and the kinds of work they might do. Prohibitions on night work for women were widespread, on the grounds that it particularly interfered with women's duties to their family and their husbands, and moreover might expose them to moral dangers. The state, it appeared, also had an interest in the sexual morality of women and in maintaining an ideal of the comfort and good order of family life.

Kelley and other reformers realized that the restriction of hours meant that women would earn less, and they attempted to rectify this by lobbying for minimum-wage laws for women. Men had already expanded the notion of rights in the basic trade-union demand for the "family wage." On the assumption that all men would eventually marry and father children, for whom they would be responsible, they both *needed* a wage high enough to support the family and had a *right* to the kind of family life that such a wage would support. In fact only skilled and organized men were in a position to achieve the "family wage," but it remained the basic goal of the trade-union movement and was sometimes described as the "American" wage, or the American standard of living, to which every workingman had a right.

The "family wage" idea worked against the woman wage earner, since the assumption was that the normal woman was part of a family, as either daughter or wife, in which she would be supported by the family wage earned by the breadwinner husband or father. Her own wage would thus always be supplemental. The woman worker was never conceived of as having to support anyone else (although many in fact did so), and if she was unfortunate enough to be on her own, all she was entitled to was a "living wage"—one that would afford the bare necessities.

Although most industrial women workers were young and single, the attention of women reformers was largely directed at the worker as mother because of concern that maternal neglect led to unhealthy and delinquent children. One solution would have been the provision of day-care services for working mothers. One of the most popular installations at the Columbian Exposition in 1893 had been the Model Day Nursery, where fairgoers could leave their children while they toured, secure in the knowledge that they were in safe and sanitary surroundings, attended by trained personnel, and supplied with up-to-date equipment and toys. The Day Nursery's most innovative aspect, though not remarked on at the time, was that this was not a charity for poor working mothers but a place where all mothers might leave their children. It was described by one admirer as "the tired mother's paradise." Since African-American women accepted outside work for mothers as a fact of life, black women's clubs were very active in founding day nurseries.

Although white women reformers did start similar enterprises for poor women workers, by the 1910s the tide of reform thinking was turning against the day nursery as a solution for the problem of working mothers. Jane Addams, who had started a day nursery at Hull House, was beginning to wonder whether its mere availability did not "tempt" a mother to outside work, to the detriment of her own health and the care of her children. Florence Kelley declared flatly that "family life is sapped in its foundations when the mothers of young children work for wages."

This commitment to domestic motherhood for working-class women, supported by a family wage for men, was representative of the attitudes of most women reformers involved with labor questions. They themselves were "new women" who had forged careers for themselves in the wide reform milieu, but when it came to the right of poor mothers to work, they faltered in their commitment to women's autonomy. Looking at the kinds of work that poor mothers did, they could not see that paid work could offer them anything of value.

Some reformers who were concerned for women's rights attempted to combine the traditional belief in domestic motherhood with a new commitment to women's independence through the idea—being promoted energetically by European activists—of "mothers' endowments." These were to be regular state payments to all mothers, designed to be generous enough that the mother did not need to work and could devote herself to her family. Because they were universal, the payments avoided the stigma of welfare. The idea also appealed to women's rights advocates because the "endowment" would give mothers an income independent of an individual man, and, like soldiers' pensions, acknowledge her service to the state. This utopian idea never got very far in the United States, but a strong campaign for a more limited mothers' pension to be paid by state governments to needy widowed mothers was launched in 1909 by a highly effective coalition of the National Congress of Mothers, the General Federation of Women's Clubs, the WCTU, and the National Consumers' League, together with prominent individuals in the reform community. Beginning in 1911, state after state passed such legislation.

Yet the actual state provisions were always penny-pinching, and there were strict conditions of eligibility. The ideal recipient was a virtuous widow. Although some states included divorced or abandoned wives, very few included unmarried mothers. The pension was not automatic on demonstration of need; each case was first examined by a case worker, and recipients were subject to ongoing surveillance. Recipients also were forbidden full-time work outside the home, but since the pensions were usually too meager to survive on, many mothers were driven to part-time or home work, both of which were among the lowest paid.

Official recognition of mothers as civic heroines came in an honorific, rather than substantive, fashion in 1914 when President Woodrow Wilson proclaimed the second Sunday in May as an official day to fly the flag and honor mothers for service to their country. The new commemorative day became a fixture in American life and a bonanza for the greeting-card and florist industries. A more bizarre tribute to motherliness was a campaign conducted by some Southern white men beginning in 1910 to erect a monument to the "old black negro mammy," touted as a model of totally selfless devotion and loyalty to her white "family." This nostalgic tribute to the Old South was advanced at a time when women, both black and white, were suggesting that "selflessness" might be abandoned, when African-American women were dressing as the Goddess of Liberty in the increas-

ingly popular Juneteenth Day celebrations commemorating the
Emancipation Proclamation, and when contemporary black
women were being relegated to the back of the streetcar and removed from first-class "ladies" cars on the railroads.

The increased visibility and assertiveness of women in public,
in business offices and city streets, in college classrooms, in labor
strikes, and in clubs and organizations with a public purpose, all
made the notion of separate spheres and the domestic retirement
of women seem less and less in tune with reality. Moreover the
remarkable political vigor of organized women and prominent
individuals in the service of social reform and state transformation in the early years of the new century made the notion of
women voting seem less extreme and more necessary. As reforming women became more intimately involved in state and local
politics, their own exclusion and lack of political clout was
brought home to them. Jane Addams, Florence Kelley, the
women of the Children's Bureau and of WTUL were all suffragists, and connected suffrage to the problems women faced in the
real world and to attempts to ameliorate them. To women who
were already thinking as "stateswomen," suffrage may not have
been at the forefront of their concerns, but it was becoming an
essential part of the new roles, the new ways of being women
they were carving out for themselves.

# 3

# Thinking About the Woman Question

The worst of being a feminist is that one has no evidence.
—Rebecca West, 1912

BY THE LATE nineteenth century women were moving into new fields and claiming new opportunities without feeling much need for an elaborate justification of what they were doing. Indeed, to act, rather than to argue on first principles, seemed less of a challenge to men and less risky.

Many thoughtful feminists, however, were drawn to the task of explaining, not just changing, women's situation. This was especially urgent since in the second half of the century the traditional argument for the inferiority of women and the rootedness of their subordination in the "nature of things" had been given vigorous new life and scientific sanction by the rise of Darwinism. Simultaneously the argument for social and civic equality for women based upon natural rights, the intellectual foundation for the first phase of the women's movement (as well as the Declaration of Independence), began to seem hopelessly old-fashioned. John Stuart Mill's *The Subjection of Women* (1869), which had been something of a bible for the first generation of women's rights activists, might, declared the editors of the *Popular Science Monthly* dismissively, have been written "two thousand years ago." The triumph of the evolutionary thought patterns ushered in by Darwin taught people to shift attention from what ought to be, and might be attained, to what *was*—the end product of a seemingly inexorable natural process of development over very long periods of time. From this essentially historical perspective, the problem to be explained for feminists was the dominance everywhere, in all societies and in all historic periods, of men over women, and their apparently exclusive role in all of civilization's advances. Wherever one looked it seemed that all achievement—in invention, in science, in art, in thought—was the achievement of men.

On the question of the subordination of women to men, many people would still merely cite the Bible. The women's movement had a mixed relationship with organized religion. Orthodox churches tended to be bastions of opposition to claims for expanded women's roles outside the home, while many liberal ministers, particularly those involved with the Social Gospel, were sympathetic. Many women also found in religion an inspiration for revolt, convinced that in going out to attack social evils, from slavery to the liquor trade, they were simply following the summons of a gospel that called alike to men and women. Thus religion could be both conservative and emancipatory. Some major leaders of the women's movement, however, were convinced that organized religion was a major obstacle to women's progress. The two most important of these were Elizabeth Cady Stanton and Matilda Joslyn Gage.

Gage was a prominent New York suffragist who largely disappeared from the record after her death in 1898 and has only recently been rediscovered. She was a collaborator in the NAWSA's *History* project, for which she wrote the first two and the last chapters of the first volume. A militant freethinker, she delighted in attacking the current conventional clichés on womanhood. "There is a word sweeter than Mother, Home, or Heaven," she insisted. "That word is Liberty." In 1893 she published her major work, *Woman, Church and State*, in which she set out her case that the Christian churches had consistently legit-imated the subordination of women to men and helped enforce it through propaganda and canon law, and at times through sheer terrorism like the great witch-hunts. More was involved than a mere conservative resistance to change; repression of women, Gage insisted, was one of the principal *functions* of churches. "The Christian Church is based upon the fact of woman servi-tude; upon the theory that woman brought sin and death into the world, and that therefore she was punished by being placed in a condition of inferiority to man. . . . This is the foundation to-day of the Christian Church."

Gage's ideas had considerable influence on Elizabeth Cady Stanton at the time she was growing bored with the narrow issue of suffrage and more and more involved in the examination of the philosophical basis of the oppression of women. Stanton con-temptuously rejected the commonly accepted truism that Chris-tianity had elevated the status of women from what it had been under paganism. It was not to religion, she wrote in a provoca-tive essay in the *North American Review* in 1885, that one should look for women's advancement, "but to material civilization, to commerce, science, art, invention, to the discovery of the art of printing, and the general dissemination of knowledge."

For a long time Stanton had been contemplating a critique of the Bible from a feminist standpoint. In 1881, to considerable criticism, a committee of male scholars had produced a Revised Version of the Bible in English. To Stanton its main defect was that the committee had not taken into account the Bible's built-in misogyny, and this omission inspired her to tackle the problem herself. In 1894, now approaching eighty, she drew together a committee to produce a commentary on selected biblical passages bearing on women. Many women she approached refused to be-come involved. Susan B. Anthony had never had much sympa-thy with Stanton's anti-clericalism and steered clear of the whole project. Like many others in the movement, she thought Stan-ton's anti-biblical crusade was flogging a dead horse. "Nobody does right or wrong because Saint Paul told them to," Anthony rebuked her friend on another occasion. "The trouble is in *ourselves to-day* not in men or books of thousands of years ago." In many ways her attitude toward religion was more thoroughly secular than Stanton's. She was content to ignore those parts of the Bible that affronted her; Stanton needed to wrestle them to the ground.

Stanton did secure the aid of a few like-minded activists, including Gage, who contributed individual comments, but most of what she dubbed the "Woman's Bible" she wrote herself. On its publication, in two volumes in 1895–1896, it met a storm of criticism—much of it from people who never read it. The title alone was enough to offend a great many people, horrified that a woman would have the effrontery to critique the holy book. At the 1896 NAWSA national convention, Anthony's protégée Rachel Foster Avery recommended that the suffrage movement go on record as disavowing any connection with the *Woman's Bible*. This was widely regarded as a wholesale repudiation of Stanton and what she stood for. Several speakers supported the old leader, and Anthony pleaded that the organization should be tolerant of all shades of opinion. Nonetheless the resolution passed handily, chiefly due to the younger women. Their displeasure seems to have stemmed not so much from affronted piety as from essentially tactical considerations; the movement could not afford to antagonize either the churches or sincerely religious women.

Stanton's main quarrel was with Genesis and the story of Adam's rib, Eve, and the apple. From this fable stemmed the insistence down the ages, internalized by women themselves, that women were the *second* sex, forever subordinate and relative to man, and that they must bear eternal punishment for having let sin and death into the world. Creation myths have power; women, Stanton felt, could never become truly emancipated and equal with men while this indictment of them was entrenched at the heart of Western culture. Now that women were coming to consciousness, it was time for the Scriptures to be rethought and reinterpreted.

One of her collaborators, the New Thought disciple Lucinda Chandler, offered an optimistic feminist slant on the story of the Fall. Perhaps, she suggested, one should see Eve, in reaching for the apple of knowledge, not as committing the original sin but as lifting the human race "out of the innocence of ignorance into truth." Stanton, however, felt it necessary to discard the whole story of a sacred creation involving the notion of sin coupled with woman, and replace it with a modern, scientific, and "progressive" account. "If . . . we accept the Darwinian theory, that the race has been a gradual growth from a lower to a higher form of life," she wrote, "and that the story of the fall is a myth, we can exonerate the snake, emancipate the woman, and reconstruct a more rational religion for the nineteenth century."

Science was in fact already becoming the "rational religion" of the nineteenth and twentieth centuries. In the early 1880s Stanton recorded "dipping into" Darwin's *Descent of Man*, along with Herbert Spencer's *First Principles*, with great satisfaction, and she always privileged "science" as a way of understanding the world. But had she plunged more deeply into Darwinian theory she would not have been so quick to link it with the emancipation of woman. In the coming century it would be "science," not religion, that constituted the most influential voice in the debate over normal sex roles and gender characteristics. The verdict of Nature, as interpreted by a largely male scientific priesthood, would prove just as authoritative as the voice of Jehovah.

However much scientists liked to think of themselves as the icily objective investigators of "facts," scientific discussion of sexual differences proceeded against a backdrop of growing female demands to enter the "male" world of higher education, professional work, and even politics. In similar fashion the examination of racial differences was given focus by political struggles over the place of African Americans in American life and the spread of European colonialism to nonwhite parts of the world.

In this period the concepts of "equality" and "rights" became scientifically suspect, as nature itself, it seemed, privileged some over others—the white over other races, men over women. As thoughtful women tried to puzzle out and explain the apparently universal subordination of women, and their small numbers of outstanding achievers, they had to contend with the new scientific theories.

Nineteenth-century scientific discussion of woman began with her general inferiority, not as a hypothesis to be tested but as an axiom to be assumed, and then worked out explanations for this inferiority according to the latest theories. Discussion centered on three areas: woman's physical inferiority—her smaller size and weaker muscles; the role of her reproductive organs and functions in her total personality and in limiting what she might do; and, most important, her mental inferiority, shown by the small number of accredited female geniuses and, most scientists confidently asserted, by everyday common experience.

One attempt to account for the mental inferiority had been the midcentury science of craniology, based on the assumption that mental ability was a function of the size and weight of the physical brain. European and American scientists measured thousands of skulls and weighed numerous brains and found that female brains were consistently smaller than those of men; the difference in brain weight between men and women was about five ounces, and the issue was often referred to as the "missing five ounces of female brain." Scientists also were interested in ranking different races on the scale of brain size and produced results showing that European male brains were on average larger than those of Asians or Africans.

The fact that the most publicized comparisons were those of sex and race demonstrates how bound up the two issues were, though white women of the period were increasingly unwilling to admit it. Even beyond brain measurements, discussions of evolution and comparative anatomy equated white women with children, "savages," and "Negroes." Woman, it was often as-

serted, in her emotionality as well as in her morphology, remained nearer to the child and to "savage races." Even her pre-
cocity—the fact that girls matured mentally and physically
earlier than boys—could be seen merely as another indication of
her basic inferiority; without the longer maturation process of
the male, the female could never match his physical or mental
abilities. Scientists often pointed out that black children were
often remarkably precocious too, up to a certain age, and then,
like white women, they stagnated.

The importance of the issue to women was reflected by the
suffragist Helen Gardener, who in 1887 rushed to question the
statistics and methods of measurement on which such studies
were based and which had appeared in the pages of the widely
read *Popular Science Monthly*. She pointed out that the figures
and authoritative opinions on smaller brain size published in
such a widely read magazine were "likely to have a wide influence upon the welfare and prospects of a large number of
women," influencing "school directors, voters, and legislators."

Brain size as a way to rank groups had the appeal of common
sense—bigger must be better—but it soon collapsed under the
weight of more precise measurement. As the difficulties of
matching physical brains with actual mental capabilities became
more apparent, craniology gradually disappeared from the forefront of science—though that missing five ounces of the female
brain continued to crop up in laymen's efforts to show conclu-
sively why women should not try to impinge on male intellectual
preserves.

A more comprehensive and lasting justification for the relega-
tion of women to secondary status emerged from the work of
Charles Darwin and his followers. By the late nineteenth century, evolution had become the reigning paradigm in thinking
about human development. In *The Origin of Species* (1859) and
*The Descent of Man* (1871), Darwin demonstrated how all life
forms evolved over long periods of time from the simple to
the complex, in an ever-ascending progression, culminating in

human beings. But it appeared that this process operated differently in males and females.

Males evolved through natural selection, the survival of the fittest in the struggle with the environment and other men. This struggle called forth and rewarded qualities of courage, strength, and intellect; human females, on the other hand, evolved through *sexual* selection, by being chosen by men. Men selected the women they would mate with, however, not for their brains or their strength but for their beauty. Thus men and women evolved via different criteria of selection, and the result was an increasing differentiation between the sexes that was rooted in natural processes. Darwin noted that the lower the animal, the less difference there was between the sexes; the higher, the greater the difference. The explanatory force of evolution was quickly applied beyond the natural world to the development of civilization, which seemed to emerge in determinate stages— from savagery to barbarism to the modern culture of the "white" Western world—and enabled a hierarchical ranking of the world's peoples on the evolutionary scale from the most backward to the most advanced. Cross-cultural investigation also seemed to show that sex distinction increased with the complexity of social and cultural development; among the "higher races" and the higher classes, there was a greater difference in body and mind between male and female than among the "lower." Increased sexual differentiation, in the direction of greater advantage for males, thus seemed to be a product both of natural evolution and of civilization.

Herbert Spencer, the most widely read and influential of nineteenth-century social scientists, in fact saw this increasing differentiation of the sexes as a primary marker of civilization. As peoples became more civilized, the division of labor between the sexes became more extreme, women became more confined to domestic space and domestic duties, and in the highest classes of the most advanced civilizations were removed from any laborious work at all. As a result, women became physically more delicate and mentally more narrow and less capable of higher forms of thought. Like Darwin, Spencer believed that in women the process of evolution was cut short earlier than in men, and he explicitly connected this "retardation" to her role in reproduction. The "cost of reproduction" in terms of the woman's energy reserves, plus the burden of child-rearing, required that, beyond a certain point, women had to sacrifice individuation and physical and mental development to the cause of perpetuating the race. Both men and women liked to speak of women's penchant for self-sacrifice; to the evolutionists this was indeed a literal sacrifice of "self." Civilization called men to become individual and superior; Nature required that women remain generic and mediocre. When Kate Chopin in her controversial 1899 novel *The Awakening* has her heroine say that she would give up her life for her children, but "I wouldn't give myself," she was challenging the whole Darwinian schema that required her to do just that.

As the details and methods of evolution were further elaborated, hierarchical sexual distinction remained a constant. Both Darwin and Spencer had believed in the inheritability of acquired characteristics, but by the turn of the century this notion had been largely discredited among scientists. It now appeared that evolution progressed by the appearance of random variations in individuals of a species. If they proved useful for survival, they were then handed on via inheritance to succeeding generations. Males appeared to be far more likely to vary from the norm than females, and this accounted for the fact that there were more male than female mental defectives, but also more male geniuses. By the end of the century, the successful entry of women into higher education made it rather less tenable to cling to a blanket theory of the mental inferiority of women. Yet for intellectual men, superiority of intellect was the last bastion likely to be surrendered. The theory of greater male "variability" saved "genius" as a male secondary sex characteristic.

By the late 1880s the idea of variability had become part of the fixed notions of popularized science in explaining the differences between the sexes. An additional explanation was offered by the influential Scottish scientist John Patrick Geddes. In his *The Evolution of Sex* (1889), Geddes traced the differences between male and female to a fundamental difference of metabolism found at every cell level. This metabolic difference produced "katabolic" males—"active, energetic, eager, passionate, variable," and "anabolic" females—"passive, conservative, sluggish and stable." These differences in metabolism led to differences in physical strength and in mental capacity; the active male developed a larger brain and greater intelligence, the passive female developed the virtues of patience and altruism. "Man thinks more, woman feels more." Women's greater capacity for feeling was necessary for their role in the production and rearing of children, into which, following Spencer, Geddes saw most of their available energy diverted. He labeled this the "reproductive sacrifice"; it was women's contribution to evolution. Geddes protested that he did not mean to privilege one metabolic pattern over the other and insisted on the essential complementarity of the two sexes in the process of evolution. But women had to realize that social roles were rooted in these fundamental natural differences and could not arbitrarily be overthrown. "What was decided among the prehistoric Protozoa," Geddes stated in a memorable phrase, "cannot be annulled by Act of Parliament."

Geddes was deeply interested in the social implications of biological science, and he aimed to present his theories in an accessible, popular style. Much of the widespread appeal of his ideas was that, while reaffirming common stereotypes of sexual difference, he offered a reformist and "progressive" attitude toward social change. In a departure from Darwin, Geddes insisted that "creation's final law is not struggle but love." Future evolutionary progress would depend on the growth of altruistic feeling in society and the substitution of cooperation for competition. Since he was convinced that women were by nature more altruistic than men, it was their moral influence that was now crucial.

While any fundamental change in sex roles was neither possible nor desirable, Geddes did think that the growing social influence of women would result in a more cooperative society.

This aspect of Geddes's thought was highly appealing to many social reformers and activist women who wanted to expand women's public roles without sacrificing the belief in their "different" and more nurturing character and general moral superiority to men. Jane Addams was much influenced by him; her book of 1902, *Democracy and Social Ethics*, took off from his evolutionary position in explaining the need for moral change to move industrial society from anachronistic competition to cooperation. Women were the natural agents of such change since "the social claim is a demand upon the emotions as well as upon the intellect." While not challenging the conventional assignment of intellect to man and emotion to woman, Addams insisted on the proper role of the emotions in moral reasoning and in the application of that reasoning to public life.

The realization that innate genetic material rather than acquired characteristics were passed on to offspring produced an increased interest in heredity. From the 1880s through the 1920s a pervasive strain of eugenic thinking developed, emphasizing the importance of genetic endowment—rather than environment, training, or education—in producing superior or inferior individuals. A number of states passed sterilization laws in the 1910s to prevent the criminal and the "feeble-minded" from reproducing their kind. Many women's rights activists were attracted to eugenics, at least in its milder forms, as a way of mitigating social problems of poverty and deviance, but it was a style of thinking that operated more naturally in the repertoire of those opposed to the woman's movement. Eugenic thinking certainly exalted the importance of the mother in the breeding of superior children, but only at the expense of precluding women from functioning as much else.

Strong eugenicists were obsessed with the idea of "race suicide" and assumed that the progress of the "race"—in this case a quite narrow meaning of white, Nordic/Anglo-Saxon—depended on the "best" women having as many children as possible. If progress was achieved through the passing on of superior hereditary traits, nothing a woman might do apart from reproducing could be of equal importance. Indeed, even her involvement in *raising* and training her children, which most women saw as their chief accomplishment and on which so much cultural praise was lavished, was of less import than her actual production. Eugenicists lamented the fact that girls of superior ability were now able to go to college, with the result that they ceased to bear many children, leaving the future America to be bred from the less able. In effect, eugenicists reiterated from a more up-to-date theoretical position the old Darwinian/Spencerian notion that women as individuals must be sacrificed to the good and perpetuation of the race. This was particularly true of the "superior" woman whose racial duty it was to sink herself in motherhood.

Evolutionism in all its varieties seemed to deny the underlying premise of the woman movement: that revolutionizing the position of women would accelerate human progress in general. Yet so all-encompassing and so intellectually compelling was the evolutionary paradigm by the end of the century that intellectual women who were striving for new roles for women had to negotiate a position within it. As early as 1875, the pioneer women's rights activist Antoinette Brown Blackwell had attempted to reexamine the Darwin/Spencer account of evolution to give women a more equal place. In her *The Sexes Throughout Nature* (1875), Blackwell had insisted that Darwin was wrong to assume that the two sexes did not keep pace with each other in evolution. Nature had indeed evolved numerous different traits between the sexes, but she insisted that these traits were of equal value to evolutionary progress.

While Blackwell valiantly tried to demonstrate that women should in no way be seen as evolutionarily "retarded," in many ways her account sounded like a scientific reworking of traditional ideas of separate but complementary characteristics and functions that would not have dismayed the most conventional believer in separate spheres. More important, Blackwell still felt compelled to accept science as arbiter: "It is to the most rigid scientific methods of investigation that we must undoubtedly look for a final and authoritative decision as to woman's legitimate nature and functions," she wrote. "Whether we approve or disapprove ... it is to Nature as umpire—to Nature interpreted by scientific methods, that we most confidently appeal." But she also thought that the sex of the scientist might make a difference in *how* Nature's decisions would be interpreted. Women, as long as they abided strictly by scientific method, should be able to correct the biases of male scientists.

The most important feminist to rework the evolutionary paradigm to support a fundamental change in women's position was Charlotte Perkins Gilman, the best-known feminist writer at the turn of the century. Gilman's feminism was firmly rooted in the evolutionary discourse of civilization so widespread in turn-of-the-century America. She believed unhesitatingly in the superiority of "white," particularly Anglo-Saxon, culture; she was deeply worried by the impact of immigration on the United States; and she saw most of the African-American population as a "problem." But her greatest concern for "white" civilization was the unevolved state of most of its womanhood, which she considered a drag on all future progress.

Gilman, who was born in 1860, was an extraordinarily prolific writer, best known today for her short story, "The Yellow Wallpaper," based upon her own nervous breakdown after the birth of her only child and the disastrous medical attempt at a cure. Yet although she wrote a good deal of fiction and poetry, she did not regard herself primarily as an artist but as a sociologist, a philosophic/scientific explicator of social evolution. She was also a follower of the Bellamyite Nationalist Movement, a Fabian socialist, and a suffragist.

Gilman's first and most important book, *Women and Econom-*

*ics* (1898), which went into nine printings by 1920 and was translated into seven languages, was subtitled "A Study of the Economic Relation Between Men and Women as a Factor in Social Evolution." Much of its impact lay in her appropriation of the evolutionist standpoint while daring to attack the sacred cows of home and motherhood. Like any philosophy that makes a popular impression, Gilman's book resonated with many readers by expressing in a more striking way their own inchoate ideas. "It seems to me that I have waited all my life to read this book," the young feminist Marie Jenney Howe wrote to Gilman. "It justifies my most cherished convictions."

Gilman discovered the key to turning the evolutionary vision to the advantage of women in the work of the sociologist Lester Frank Ward. In his 1888 essay, "Our Better Halves," Ward had rescued evolution for women by offering what he called a "gynaecocentric theory" of human development. Woman, Ward maintained, was not a secondary creature, evolved purely for procreation, as Darwin and Spencer implied; rather, it was the female who was at the center of evolution. The male had developed initially only for the purpose of fertilization. Over the course of human evolution these secondary males had become dominant over women and outstripped them in muscular and brain power, but women retained a vital evolutionary role as the "race type." Women preserved and transmitted to their children the essential traits of their respective races.

Many women jumped at Ward's reversal of the priority of Adam and Eve, and Gilman made it the foundation of her philosophy. She agreed with Spencer that women had been retarded in their development, but she denied that this was a necessary concomitant of the reproductive sacrifice; rather, it was a result of the evolution of male dominance through changes in sexual selection. Primitive females had originally "selected" the males and had chosen for strength, bravery, and brains because they found these qualities attractive and, in their mates, useful for their own survival. But at some point men, like Frankenstein's monster, had turned upon their creators, used their superior strength and cunning to subdue them, and then wrested away the prerogative of sexual selection. Men then selected women for the traits *they* found useful and attractive: good looks, physical weakness, docility, an anxiety to please, and the willingness to be dominated.

Continually bred for physical and mental weakness, women had over time become totally economically dependent upon men. Women did not actually earn their living through their "home-making" activities; the amount and quality of the food, shelter, and clothing the housewife received depended entirely on the earning capacity of her husband, and in fact bore an inverse relation to the actual amount of housework she performed. Like later sociobiologists, Gilman liked to draw analogies between animal and human behavior, and used them to show how far the human female had departed from the independence and courage of her animal ancestors. She pointed out that all adult animals, male and female, got their own food, and among predators it was the mother that hunted down prey for her offspring. All this was reversed among human beings, the only species in which the female normally depended upon the male for sustenance: "He is," she noted laconically, "her food supply."

Gilman acknowledged that the dominance of the "katabolic" variable male, with his abundant energy, aggressiveness, and inventiveness, had produced the high level of modern civilization, but the costs had been considerable and by now outweighed the benefits. The aggressiveness and competitiveness of what she later called the "androcentric" culture had by the dawn of the twentieth century become a positive danger to civilization. It had to be modified in the direction of cooperation. As for women, their economic dependence had corrupted as well as enslaved them. Domestic confinement to the home had cut women off from all the progressive activities that continued to improve the male. Men had developed the capacity for specialized, interdependent, collaborative work, and from this the extraordinary productiveness and inventiveness of the modern economy had emerged. Women, on the other hand, confined to the home, worked in isolation at numerous unspecialized tasks, usually performed in much the same fashion as their grandmothers.

Unfortunately the dysgenic criteria by which men selected mates had combined with the debasing and narrowing environment of domestic life to make women progressively more incompetent. The sexes were indeed becoming more and more different over time, as Spencer had maintained, but Gilman could not find this progressive. Confinement to the home made woman physically weaker, mentally sluggish, and morally stunted; she had become cowardly, narrow, and selfish, unable to look beyond the interests of her own narrow world. Gilman did not dispute that women's most important task was the bearing of superior children. Indeed, her 1914 utopian novel, *Herland*, is about an isolated, peaceful, cooperative, all-female society which reproduces through parthenogenesis and is organized entirely around maternity and the nurture of children. The problem with motherhood in the real world, however, according to Gilman, was that most mothers were not very good at it. Their narrow characters and excessive concentration on their own family affairs equipped women poorly to mold the characters of their children. And the home, that sacred cow of domestic ideology, was the inefficient and expensive temple of an outmoded individualism, the prison of women, and certainly not a suitable place for bringing up children. "Only as we live, think, feel, and work outside the home," Gilman wrote, "do we become humanly developed, civilized, socialized."

Ironically, precisely because human social evolution had worked to specialize women to domestic and maternal—specifically sexual—functions, they had become inferior mothers. By becoming more "woman," women had become progressively less human. Yet in this there was no long-term evolutionary advantage for the human race as a whole. The inferior characteristics of woman, bred through the combination of sexual selection and environmental modification, were passed on to her children, male as well as female. The "retardation" of half the human race, in the end, served to drag down the whole of it.

Like all female evolutionists, Gilman refused to believe that the current state of affairs, even in the most highly evolved Anglo-American world, was the final stage of development. However useful the subordination of women to men may have been to evolution, the next progressive stage would depend upon the emancipation of women. In order to improve as mothers, not to mention as human beings, women had to become economically self-supporting and get out of the house. They would not fully develop physically, mentally, or even morally until they were part of the interdependent world of "human work," which she defined as "specialized activity in some social function—any art, craft, trade or profession that serves society."

For this to take place, the material organization of family life would have to be reformed. For the middle-class housewife, live-in domestic servants were disappearing; nor was it desirable to bring them back. Gilman suggested that almost all housework should be done by well-paid professionals, working regular hours. Certain tasks like laundry and cooking should be done outside the home altogether. The family no longer made its own beer or spun its own cloth; why should it cook its own dinner? Gilman insisted that she was not advocating cooperative living. She was aware that the many experiments on these lines had mostly failed. She had far more confidence in the impersonal co-operation embodied in the division of labor of modern commerce. "This is the true line of advance; making a legitimate, human business of housework; having it done by experts instead of by amateurs; making it a particular social industry instead of a general feminine function."

In a 1904 magazine article, Gilman produced an elaborate plan and budget for a whole city block that would house professional and business families, in which the wife as well as the husband would work outside the home. All cleaning and cooking, from a central kitchen, would be done by professionals working for the collectivity. On-site professional child care would also be provided, not only to enable mothers to work outside the home but because most women would probably be better mothers if they were less constantly with their children; and children would become less self-centered by spending more time apart from overanxious and overfond mothers. A Gilman disciple, the socialist Henrietta Rodman of New York, actually proposed a viable project for an apartment house along these lines, but she could never get the funding to build it.

Gilman's most valuable contribution to feminist thinking was less her evolutionist adaptations than her recognition that the role of the married woman and mother was the crux of the woman question. The college girl, the young emancipated New Woman, and the mature woman who had deliberately forgone marriage to devote herself to a career or to reform work might be the vanguard of women's new roles, but most women would always marry and have children. It was in *their* future, in their ability to function in the world as well as the home, that the fate of women lay. "Until 'mothers' earn their livings," she pointed out, "'women' will not." Gilman also incorporated two major ideas that were central to most feminist intellectuals who thought about the woman question: the conviction that, desirable though it was to have the vote, economic independence must be at the core of women's emancipation; and the belief that at some point in the far distant past, Something had Happened, that the subordination of women to men was a historical development (even if a very long-standing one) rather than a natural given, and that it had now become exceptionally dysfunctional, not only for women but for society as a whole.

The nineteenth century gradually became accustomed to thinking in terms of very long periods of time, extending beyond known history to the misty realm of prehistory and myth. One example of this kind of thinking that was becoming particularly popular by the 1880s was the idea of the matriarchate. The Swiss Johann J. Bachofen, in an 1861 book, *Myth, Religion, and Mother-Right*, had postulated a very early prehistoric society dominated by women, with kinship based upon matrilineal inheritance, that had eventually been overthrown by a revolt of men who then asserted their own dominance.

The idea of a woman-dominated society had obvious attractions for women's rights activists, even though Bachofen had not actually portrayed the matriarchate as a golden age. He regarded it rather as an aspect of the "childhood" of the human race, and its eventual overthrow by patriarchy had meant the triumph—necessary for civilization and progress—of rationality and the spirit over instinct and nature. Still, he did rather wistfully envision "an air of tender humanity" as having permeated "the culture of the matriarchal world." This was a social climate that to most women correlated to what they assumed a woman-directed society would be like.

By the last quarter of the nineteenth century, the new and rapidly expanding field of anthropology was supplying evidence of the diversity of human social arrangements. It even described societies that, if not exactly dominated by women, were nonetheless matrilineal in family organization, and where women seemed to enjoy a particularly high status. The work of the American anthropologist Lewis Henry Morgan confirmed the existence of matrilineal descent among "primitive" peoples, not just in the ancient past but among the contemporary Iroquois. Like Bachofen, Morgan also linked the overthrow of matriarchy with the rise of civilization, the patriarchal family, and the development of private property. Friedrich Engels, in his *The Origin of the Family, Private Property, and the State* (1884), did so too, describing the process in apocalyptic terms as "the world-historical defeat of the female sex." It was a defeat that, linked as it was to the rise of private property, also ushered in a long era of general inequality and injustice. Engels acknowledged that patriarchy

had been a necessary stage in the development of higher civilization, but he predicted that it would in turn be superseded by a
still higher stage: socialism.

Other students of anthropology and prehistory now disputed
Spencer's claim that civilization was entirely and originally a
male construct. Otis Tufton Mason, a pioneer ethnologist at the
Smithsonian Institution, in his *Woman's Share in Primitive Culture* (1899), insisted that while primitive men had occupied
themselves with war or the hunt, women were industriously laying the foundations of civilized life through the development of
agriculture, the domestication of animals, and the use of tools,
pottery, baskets, and fibers for clothing. However far distant it
was, women could point to a past of considerable achievement.

The concept of the matriarchate soon became part of the general consciousness of the women's rights community. The pioneers Elizabeth Cady Stanton and Matilda Joslyn Gage accepted
the literal existence of a historical matriarchate and gave it a central role in their thinking. Its major appeal was that it seemed to
demonstrate that patriarchy, the dominance of men over women,
was not necessarily rooted in nature; it was a historical development that might shift again. The matriarchate gave women a
"usable past" but one of which they had been despoiled; and as
every nationalist movement knows, to be deprived of something
once possessed is a greater spur to rage and revolt than the mere
hope of gaining something entirely new.

Another widely accepted but shorter-term historical perspective on women's position pointed to the impact of the industrial
revolution. The economic changes wrought by industrialization
offered what became a favorite argument as to why women's
roles needed to be expanded. The household, far from always
being a purely domestic retreat, had once been a unit of production, particularly in textiles and food preservation, an integral
part of the general economy. Seventeenth- and eighteenth-
century wives and daughters had been fully engaged in this vital
economic activity; they had not been mere consumers and de-

pendents. Modern industrialization, however, had taken most of those productive tasks out of the home and into the factory, leaving wives with the unrewarding drudgery of household maintenance and daughters with makework. To Spencer and his followers, this removal of women from productive work in favor of dedication to domesticity was a mark of progress out of barbarism. But to many in the woman's movement it seemed rather that modern life had robbed women of the self-respect—and the respect of others—that came from being an active and recognized producer in the economy. Even the United States Census classified wives as "dependents"; only those with a paying job outside the home were classed as having an "occupation."

The assumption that women had lost status along with a useful economic role was a direct challenge to the belief that economic dependency was the natural condition of women, and that the presence of women as wage earners in the work world was an unfortunate aberration of immature capitalism, eventually to be cured by the triumph of the family wage which would enable male workers to keep their womenfolk at home. To the contrary, asserted defenders of women workers, in following their old productive tasks out of the home into the factory and workshops, or even into the office and the professions, women were doing nothing unnatural or revolutionary but were merely riding with the flow of historical evolution. Moreover, in regaining their productive role women might regain the status they had presumably once had and lost. A similar point was being made in the same period by the African-American educator Booker T. Washington, who was assuring black men that by acquiring economically useful skills they would earn the recognition and respect of whites.

The belief that status is linked to economic utility is morally appealing but hardly backed by much empirical evidence. Still, the notion that the modern middle-class housewife had become unproductive, and that in the long run this put her in an untenable position, had considerable currency. Unlike most house-

wives, who were more likely to think of themselves as over-
rather than underworked, feminists tended to assume that wives'
"maintenance work" in the home was not as "useful" as the real
production of goods. Nor could they accept with equanimity the
argument made by the sociologist Thorstein Veblen in his *Theory
of the Leisure Class* (1899) that in vicariously and conspicuously
consuming leisure for her overworked businessman husband,
the "idle" wife was in fact performing the quite useful (to him)
function of publicly demonstrating his wealth and status.

The idea of the redundancy of middle- and upper-class Western women was put starkly by the South African writer Olive
Schreiner, who rivaled Gilman as the most famous feminist
writer of the early twentieth century. Schreiner too was steeped
in evolutionary ideas and, like Gilman, saw the movement for
women's emancipation as part of the progressive movement of
evolution. Those who opposed it were caught in a cultural lag
and did not appreciate the inevitable logic of modern industrial
civilization. In her *Women and Labor* (1911), she devoted half the
book to an explication of what she bluntly called female "parasitism": the condition of performing no "active conscious social
labor," being reduced "like the field-bug, to the passive exercise
of her sex functions alone.... The result of this parasitism has
invariably been the decay in vitality and intelligence of the female."

Through most of human history, only the wives and daughters of the extremely rich had been thus affected, but Schreiner
was convinced that within the next fifty years, industrialization,
modernization, and labor-saving machinery would bring even
women of the poorest classes into the same position. Even
women's reproductive function was declining in utility. Since the
new industrial economy required fewer workers, it was no
longer necessary to the economy that women bear many children. Thus the threat of sexual parasitism was emerging as the
eventual fate of *all* women.

The movement of women into occupations outside the home

was an instinctive response to these developments by a few of the most "advanced" women, and was thus "essentially but one important phase of a general modification which the whole of modern life is undergoing." It represented a recognition not merely of the oppressive nature of dependent domesticity but of its increasing redundancy. If the mass of women failed to lay effective claim to the world of work outside the home, Schreiner warned, it would be quite possible for men to "absorb the entire fields of intellectual and highly trained manual labor," leaving women to exist merely as "prostitutes, as kept mistresses or as kept wives," sunk into "a condition of complete and helpless sex-parasitism." The only way for women to escape this fate was to proclaim with Schreiner: "We claim, to-day, all labor for our province!"

Schreiner did not see women's right to work outside the home as competing with men. But many men did regard the encroachment of women into so many areas that had once been male preserves as inevitably leading to competition between the sexes—a competition, some warned, that would be fatal to women. The implication was that men and women could coexist peaceably only as long as they did not compete, and the only way to avoid competition was to remain in separate spheres. But to most feminists—certainly to Gilman and Schreiner—the more that men and women could undertake the same kinds of work, the more they would understand each other. The current extreme division of labor between men and women forced them to live in separate worlds; apart from brief moments of sexual passion and a common interest in their children, they had little to say to each other. The next stage in evolution would bring what Schreiner called a "great movement of the sexes toward each other . . . common occupations, common interests, common ideals," would all bring a greater "emotional sympathy" between men and women. There was thus a fundamental difference between feminists and their opponents as to whether harmony between the sexes depended on keeping them mostly apart in character, nature, and occupation, or on making them more nearly alike, both in what they did and what they were. Schreiner was not afraid to call her ideal woman not only "active" but "virile."

While theorists like Gilman and Schreiner were thinking in terms of grand metahistorical schema, by the early twentieth century the new social sciences were producing researchers who were preparing to put the question of the relative abilities of the sexes to empirical test. Women in intellectual professions could not afford to accept the attribution of moral superiority as a consolation for mental inferiority. In the 1910s new challenges to the supposition of lower female intelligence began to emerge from women researchers at the University of Chicago, an institution that was young, well endowed, progressive, and remarkably open to new disciplines like sociology and to the employment of women.

In 1900 Helen Thompson, a graduate student working with the philosopher John Dewey at Chicago, decided to test the commonly accepted scientific judgments on the relative mental abilities of the sexes by the new technique of taking precise measurements of various indices from a small sample population. She used a group of matched male and female undergraduates, from the same socioeconomic background and level of education, and tested them on a number of traits including motor skills, sensory perception, puzzle solving, and general information. She found the differences between her male and female test subjects to be much less than was generally supposed. And it seemed to her that most of the differences she did find could more easily be attributed to environmental causes than innate characteristics.

Most important, instead of averaging, Thompson graphed her results, demonstrating a high degree of overlap in the abilities of men and women, even though, in accordance with the accepted belief, more men turned up at the top and the bottom of the scale. Thus her experiments got away from the habit of dichotomous thinking about the abilities of the sexes. They showed a wide variation of ability among individuals, even of the same social and educational level, but individual variation seemed to have little correlation with sex. Gender alone was certainly not much of a predictor of the capacities of any individual man or woman. The import for the future of women, she concluded, was to deny that science should be the arbiter of women's fate. "The question of the future development of the intellectual life of women," she wrote, "is one of social necessities and ideals, rather than of the inborn psychological characteristics of sex."

The import of Thompson's research was immediately seized on by the Chicago sociologist William I. Thomas, who realized its implications for the study of racial differences as well as sex. In his own earlier work on sex differences, he had fully accepted Geddes's katabolic/anabolic distinction as determining psychological differences of sex. Women, he had concluded then, remained "intermediate in development between the child and the man," and the "brain of woman taken as a whole is uniformly in a more or less embryonic condition." By 1907, however, Thomas began to emphasize the impact of environmental causes in shaping the mind, which he described in 1907 as "nothing but a means of manipulating the outside world." Besides considerable contact with Jane Addams and Hull House, Thomas spent much time in the immigrant neighborhoods of Chicago and was struck by the ways in which the newcomers adapted to the massive changes in their lives. If mind developed in response to new and unaccustomed stimuli, he reasoned, differences in mental capacities and characteristics between men and women were likely to be the result of social arrangements that forced a narrower range of activity and focus of attention upon women than upon men. By 1910 he could state: "No-one is altogether male or female. The life of men and women corresponds more than it differs."

Surveying the field in 1910, Helen Thompson concluded that discussion seemed to be shifting from "a biological to a sociological interpretation of the mental characteristics of sex." A new environmentalism was emerging to dethrone the determining effects of the prehistoric protozoa. In a society in flux, in a fast-moving world, character and ability had to be seen as plastic and adaptable. Thomas brought to the fore the molding effect of the *immediate* and changing environment rather than the remote, prehistoric past. Although Thomas and Thompson did not make the modern distinction between sex and gender, they were certainly insisting on the same phenomenon: that the human being was born male or female but learned to be masculine or feminine. That learning process was so all-encompassing from birth that it became in effect a "second nature."

In 1912 a Chicago graduate student, Jessie Taft, wrote a dissertation on the social psychology of women in which she asserted that in so far as the psychology of women was markedly different from that of men, it was because boys and girls learned from an early age the behavior and personal traits thought suitable to their sex. Taft was building upon the idea of the "social self" that was being put forward by her mentor George Herbert Mead: personality was developed in the course of interaction with those around one. Women developed subordinate personalities because that was what everyone from the earliest days expected of them.

Taft brought her interest in psychology to her discussion of the woman movement in her 1916 book, *The Woman Movement from the Point of View of Social Consciousness*, in which she insisted on the vital psychological dimension of emancipation for women. No fundamental change in woman's social position was likely until both men and women learned to regard desirable qualities such as courage, rationality, and compassion as ungendered and equally open to development by both sexes. Nor could women ever attain their full potential while isolated in the home from the main currents of modern social life. "The individual is not economically or morally free," she insisted, "except when he is able to express himself, to realize his ends through the common life."

Edward Thorndike, an educational psychologist at Columbia University, who became a leader of the new movement for mental testing, agreed that women's characteristics of mind and per-

sonality seemed to be the result of education rather than innate.
He also agreed that there was little mental difference between
the average man and the average woman, but he clung to the
idea of greater variability in males. This meant that not only
were 97 percent of known geniuses that had ever lived males, but
97 percent always *would* be males. This was not just a sop to male
vanity; it had practical consequences for education and the professions. "The education of women for such professions as administration, statesmanship, philosophy or scientific research,"
Thorndike wrote in 1906 ("Sex in Education"), "is far less
needed than education for such professions as nursing, teaching,
medicine or architecture, where the average level is essential."
His dismissive dumping of medicine and architecture into the
"average" pool certainly illuminates why male physicians and ar-
chitects were trying desperately to assert the virility of their occupations.

Thorndike's student Leta Hollingworth, who went on to a
career as chief of psychology at Bellevue Hospital in New York,
was not ready to accept her mentor's position and took on the
conceptual assumptions behind the variability theory. She felt
that scientists too easily relied on unexamined assumptions and
general folklore when dealing with the relative abilities of the
sexes. And this was dangerous, not only for the pursuit of scientific truth but because of the ways in which scientific ideas were
used in public policy and affected social attitudes. Scientists, she
warned, should "guard against accepting as an established fact
about human nature a doctrine that we might expect to find in
use as a means of social control."

One of the scientific "truisms" that Hollingworth challenged
was the assumption that menstruation incapacitated women
once a month, requiring physical rest and even causing mental
derangement. When she gave a group of female students a series
of mental and motor tests regularly over several months and correlated their scores with their menstrual calendar, she found no
effect whatsoever on how well they did. Rheta Dorr, in a 1915

*New York Times* article entitled "Is Woman Biologically Barred from Success?" could draw on this research for her emphatic "No!" Hollingworth's findings were corroborated by Clelia Duel Mosher, a physician who undertook several studies of menstruation among college women over a period of thirty years between 1890 and 1920. Mosher also found a considerable change over time in the degree of menstrual problems reported by young women, and revealed how dramatic the effects of quite short-term environmental changes could be. In 1894, when fifteen pounds of petticoats hung from a corseted waist measuring on average twenty inches, 80 percent of the college women she interviewed reported experiencing some menstrual problems; by 1916, when clothes had become much lighter and waists considerably larger, 68 percent were problem free.

By the early twentieth century the interest in correlating qualities of mind and personality to physiological structure was being superseded by an interest in the precise measurement of intelligence through testing. In 1905 the Frenchman Alfred Binet developed the idea of the intelligence quotient—IQ—a notion taken up enthusiastically by American psychologists who developed numerous tests to measure it. The most famous of these was the Stanford-Binet test of 1916. By World War I there was widespread skepticism about the idea that women were becoming increasingly more differentiated from men through heredity, sexual selection, and acquired characteristics, and by 1918 references to sex differences in intelligence were going out of style in psychology. The war gave a great boost to mental testing, but the target population then was the body of all-male recruits, so that the tests measured differences in cognitive ability among *men*, and the results were used to show the relative mental inferiority of new immigrants rather than women.

Even as it began to appear that mental and psychological differences between the sexes were less clear-cut and less immutable than had traditionally been thought, the argument against any fundamental change in the position of women seemed to be shifting away from their capacities, however measured. Much was now made of the compatibility of women's new roles with other strongly entrenched and treasured values—especially the well-being of the family. In 1909 the *American Journal of Sociology* devoted an entire issue to a conference on "The Family." The discussion revolved around the question of whether the "family" as an institution could survive modern conditions, in particular how far it could survive the modernization of women. The general tenor of the articles was that while modern innovations like the higher education of women, easier divorce, and women's work outside the home were all probably inevitable, motherhood in particular might not be compatible with the greater individuation of women. The lower birthrate among the educated classes remained a concern, and the growth in the divorce rate seemed to stem from selfish demands for individual happiness, particularly on the part of women. The Harvard philosopher Hugo Munsterberg was quoted without comment: "From whatever side we look at it, the self-assertion of woman exalts her at the expense of the family—perfects the individual but injures society." For the rest of the twentieth century, the assumed tension between the freedom and equality of women and the well-being of the family would remain the most frequent and effective argument against fundamental change for women.

# 4

# Feminism and the Problem of Sex

We have talked enough of women's emancipation. Let us begin
to live it. No philosophy carries such conviction as the personal
life.—quoted in Katherine Anthony, *Feminism in Germany and
Scandinavia,* 1915

Unfortunately we fall in love, and Feminism must take that into
consideration.—Dora Russell, in an interview with Crystal
Eastman, 1926

THE PROBLEM modern women now had to face, wrote
the sociologist/anthropologist Elsie Clews Parsons in her 1914
*Journal of a Feminist,* "is primarily a psychological problem. How
are women to live *with* men, not *without* men like the ruthless
fighters for institutional freedom, and not in the old way *through*
men." "Living *with* men" involved the creation of new modes of
etiquette and interaction for men and women in the public,
extrafamilial world of work, but most of all it involved working
out new relationships within the private world of marriage.

By the turn of the century many "new women" profoundly
distrusted marriage; indeed, it was often their reaction to the
lives of married women of their mothers' generation that had
first propelled many into women's rights activism. For too many

women, marriage seemed to mean a life of drudgery, invalidism, a dwindling of personality, a submergence in others—a black hole of the self. Rheta Dorr recalled being struck, during childhood games in an old cemetery, by all the tombstones of New England worthies bearing the addendum: "And ———, wife of the above." At least as she remembered it, she vowed then and there that she would never end up as merely "And Rheta, wife of the above."

"It is a problem that we have undertaken," says the fictional Dr. Zay to the man she has just agreed to marry without abandoning her medical career. Elizabeth Stuart Phelps's novel *Doctor Zay* was written in 1882, one of several novels about women doctors of that period. It was unusual in suggesting that the heroine could "have it all"—a career and marriage—but the story stops before having to explain how this would work in practice. In the 1880s most women who developed a commitment to professional work did not, in fact, marry. Rather, they saw themselves quite consciously as being faced with a decisive life choice: marriage-and-children or a career. The scientist Alice Hamilton sternly told a friend in 1890 that it was foolish for a woman to think she could have both: "The proper state of society is one in which a woman is free to choose between an independent life of celibacy or a life given up to childbearing and rearing the coming generation." Although the choice might seem stark, Hamilton's generation saw the glass as half full, not half empty; the choice presented not so much a cruel dilemma as an opening of options. The first generation of professional women felt themselves privileged because, unlike their mothers' generation, they *did* have a choice between "an independent life" and conventional marriage. Many also developed long-lasting domestic partnerships with other women that may or may not have had a sexual component, and they found a satisfying emotional life in homosocial communities of women.

By the early twentieth century, however, fewer "new women" were ready to abandon the expectation of heterosexual love and children, and were beginning to resent the idea that they *had* to choose when men did not. As late as 1910 only just over 12 percent of professional women were married, but by 1920 this had risen to 20 percent. If the "new woman" was going to marry, however, it would not be for economic security or because she had no other choice in life, but for real intimacy and companionship. Of marriage she would ask less materially but far more psychologically. And she would want to hang on to the economic independence and strong sense of self that she had forged through education and work. As Crystal Eastman, one of the *new* new women of the early twentieth century, noted, the modern woman wanted money and work of her own, and some means of self-expression. "But she wants husband, home, and children, too. How to reconcile these two desires in real life, that is the question." Would it ever really be possible for women, in the words of the suitor of one prominent woman, to "marry like a man," that is to marry not for economic support or to find an identity and a life in another, but to add marriage to an already full and developed life?

"We all determined to combine marriage and careers, somehow," recalled Elizabeth Stanton's granddaughter, Nora Stanton Blatch, of her female classmates at Cornell at the beginning of the century. "It would be hard, but it could be done." It did turn out to be hard. As the novelist Mary Austin explained grimly in her autobiography why possibilities for marriage with compatible intellectual or artistic men all fell through: "One or the other of us would have to make sacrifices; and it was always sufficiently plain that I should have to be the one."

We can take as examples three early-twentieth-century "high flyers," all of whom married with considerable disruption to their careers. Alice Freeman had become president of Wellesley at the age of twenty-seven and enjoyed a brilliant few years there. When she married Professor Herbert Palmer of Harvard in 1887 at the age of thirty-two, he, she, and the Wellesley governing board all assumed that she would resign. She did, and though she worked out a new career for herself as an influential educational consultant, she never again attained the same degree of power and prestige.

Since women tended to marry men older than themselves, and thus more advanced in their careers and with higher earning power, it usually seemed to make sense that the couple would move to follow *his* career opportunities. Dorothy Reed, for example, with an M.D. from Johns Hopkins, had a stellar career in medical research until she married in her thirties and followed her academic husband to Wisconsin. There she found few opportunities to practice medicine and none for research. She too carved out a new career for herself in public health work, lecturing widely on child and maternal health care. When her husband accepted a new position in Washington, D.C., she became closely associated with the work of the Children's Bureau.

Helen Thompson, the brilliant Chicago graduate student who had done pioneering experimental work on mental differences between the sexes, married a physician and resigned her academic position at Mount Holyoke to follow him to various posts abroad. Even when her husband returned to the United States and an appointment on the medical faculty of the University of Cincinnati, she was not able to get an academic job. Helen Thompson Wooley also evolved a new career, as a child development specialist, reformer, and suffrage worker. As with Dorothy Reed, marriage had not prevented her from having a career, but it had deflected her from having the one she had envisaged and started out with.

Perhaps the new careers these women patched together for themselves were just as socially useful and interesting as their earlier ones, but marriage had certainly deflected their natural trajectory in a way that it would not have done for a man. Dorothy Reed Mendenhall, in particular, was always acutely conscious that her former mentors at Johns Hopkins were disappointed and felt that all her expensive training had been wasted.

The advent of children, of course, made juggling a career even more difficult, but giving it up did not necessarily bring ease and contentment. Lydia Commander, a feminist who in 1907 wrote *The American Idea* in explanation and defense of the modern small family, pointed out that the woman who had worked before marriage had acquired a taste for freedom. In the earliest days of her marriage, she could continue to enjoy that freedom along with companionship with her husband. "Into this life of freedom children come as a disturbing element." Not only was her liberty curtailed, but she could not be her husband's companion in the same way. "He goes on growing mentally and she falls behind." She quoted one correspondent who had been a businesswoman but gave up her career upon marriage. She now had three children and felt not only "stunted, dwarfed and narrowed. I have been shut right off as if I took mental chloroform."

Many friends of women's emancipation urged them to resist the pressures to give up outside work when they married. When in 1920 his daughter-in-law asked the Chicago philosopher George Herbert Mead whether she should give up her plans to go to medical school after the birth of her son, he advised her strongly to persevere, for "being a wife and a mother is no longer a calling in itself." He urged her to attend medical school part-time and endorsed nursery schools which were "removing the child from the obsession of maternal devotion to the great advantage of the child." The junior Meads were affluent enough that they could afford domestic help, and Irene Tufts Mead did go to medical school (though it took her nine years to graduate) and became a practicing psychiatrist.

Mead's colleague at Chicago, William I. Thomas, rallied women to remember that while childbearing might interrupt their work, the "important point in all work is not to be uninterrupted but to begin again." This was sound advice, though probably few women would have been convinced by his added remark that childbearing was "not more significant, when viewed in the aggregate and from the standpoint of time, than the interruptions of the work of men by their in-and-out-of-door games." Thomas, indeed, thought that both education and out-side work for women would make for more all-round happier marriages; they would be remedies, he wrote in his 1907 *Sex and Society,* for the "pettiness, ill health, and unserviceableness of modern woman." Much of the strain of modern marriages, Thomas believed, came from the fact that wives with no other outlet demanded a constant attention from husbands that busy men were unable to give.

Elsie Clews Parsons felt that employers ought to be willing to offer half- or three-quarter days to their employees who were mothers. This, she noted in her *Journal of a Feminist,* was the "only vital question left in the subject of women as wage earners. It is or ought to be a vital question to feminists, to econo-mists. . . ." Her fellow feminist, Katherine Anthony, insisted in 1915 that the marriage and/or career question should not be re-garded as a personal dilemma but as a "task in organization, the collective organization of women's lives." But "society" did not (and still does not) assume this as a collective task. Rather, most people regarded it as a woman's problem, which each woman would have to solve in her own way. It had to be tackled one man, one child, one job at a time, and often by cobbling together a ramshackle framework of an increasingly hard-to-find "trea-sure" of a domestic help, a helpful and nearby mother or sister, and the serendipitous discovery of a new progressive nursery school. And, above all, a supportive and cooperative husband.

By the early twentieth century some husbands had indeed become "new men" and were remarkably supportive of their wives' ambitions. The economist Wesley Mitchell, who in his courtship of Lucy Sprague had declared how proud he was of her for "marrying like a man," supported her in becoming a leading authority on early childhood education. Despite his own demanding career, he took over a good deal of the actual business of rearing their children. Leta Hollingworth's husband not only continually supported his wife's work but financed her graduate studies from his own meager academic salary. The pianist Amy

Beach's marriage ended her concert career, but it was her husband who prodded and encouraged her into becoming a notable composer. The second husband of Carrie Chapman Catt, who led the suffrage forces to victory in 1919, provided generous financial support to her suffrage work.

Unfortunately it was not always possible to tell in advance how accommodating a husband would turn out to be. A liberal ideology, even a commitment to the rights of women in the abstract, did not guarantee accommodation in the particular. The prominent progressive reformer Frederic C. Howe, for example, married Marie Jenney, the young Unitarian minister who several years before had written to Charlotte Gilman declaring her discipleship. In his autobiography, *Confessions of a Reformer*, Howe acknowledged his failings as a progressive husband. Even though intellectually he believed in personal freedom and women's rights, his instincts wanted "my old-fashioned picture of a wife rather than an equal partner." It was not until the couple moved from Ohio to New York City and settled in Greenwich Village that Howe endorsed, and even encouraged, his wife to take on a public role. But, as he confessed ruefully, "I had taken many years out of her life."

Reflecting on the situation, Howe noted the importance of "disapproval by one's class or the society in which one lives." In Cleveland "women did not take part in things. . . . They did not earn their own living. That was a public admission of failure by the husband." In New York, on the other hand, "women of distinction" were involved in the suffrage movement, and "no more notice was taken of a woman in work than a man." This new environment enabled Howe to modify his prejudices. He suspected that he was rather typical of men of his class and progressive politics. "I have sometimes doubted whether many of the men who spoke and worked for the equality of women really desired it. Intellectually yes, but instinctively no; they clung as did I to the propertied instinct, to economic supremacy, to the old idea of

marriage, in which all that a woman got she got through peti-
tioning for it."

Given the difficulties, it may not be surprising that, while the
divorce rate as a whole doubled between 1900 and 1920, professional women who married were considerably more likely to divorce than other women. Nora Stanton Blatch, who had started
out with such high hopes of combining marriage and career, did
maintain a successful career as a civil engineer, but her marriage
quickly ended in divorce.

The increasing emphasis on the question of combining career
and marriage among a small but articulate and visible segment
of urban women marked a new phase in the development of the
women's movement. And sometime around 1909 or so a new
word appeared to describe this new departure: "feminism." It
was adopted from the French and was used by its advocates to
connote a more radical, but perhaps more fundamental, aspect of
the broad women's movement than suffrage alone. By February
1913 *McClure's Magazine* thought it necessary to recognize feminism, on the grounds that "no movement of this century is more
significant or more deep-rooted than the movement to readjust
the social position of women." The editors appointed Inez Milholland, a young and rather glamorous suffragist, to conduct a
new Women's Department. She depicted feminism not as a junior offshoot but rather as the "deeper parent" of the suffragist
movement, and entitled her first article "The Liberation of a
Sex."

"Liberation" as a defining theme of feminism, rather than a
focus on civil rights or women's claim to a larger voice in civic
affairs, linked it to the earliest nineteenth-century beginnings
of the woman movement, when there had been a strong sense of
emergence and the casting off of shackles. The consciousness of
promoting a revolution in women's relation to the world, to
men, and to themselves, repressed in the mainstream suffrage
movement by the grind of tactical planning and minutiae,

reemerged in the small groups of mainly young and well-educated women who began to identify themselves as "feminists." There was thus some overlap, and also a conscious distancing, between the two movements. While they accepted the public goals of the women's suffrage movement, feminists also consciously distinguished themselves from the older suffragists, whom they saw as too "Victorian," too heavily moralistic, too repressed—and too superficial in their analysis of women's needs. Feminists believed in full citizenship for women, and thus suffrage; they also believed that women must become self-supporting, and so they believed in paid work. But above all they believed that liberation demanded an inner revolution in women's psyches, a willingness to take risks, to flout conventions, to assert equality in the state, on the job, and in their personal relationships.

This meant above all, as Elsie Parson's *Journal* remark indicated, their personal and sexual relationships with men. While the older generation of suffragists had rebelled against a familial woman's domestic culture that they perceived as a deadly mixture of drudgery and trivia, the new young feminists were also rebelling against the earnest homosocial and asexual women's culture of their elders in the movement. Their more open attitude toward heterosexuality, and their readiness to discuss it, was likely to provide plentiful ammunition to the opponents of suffrage. Many women involved in the mainstream suffrage movement were thus rather careful to steer clear of "feminism" for ideological, tactical, and personal reasons. As one feminist put it: "All feminists are suffragists, but not all suffragists are feminists."

In 1912 a group of thirtyish women in New York City organized themselves into a club called Heterodoxy. Founded by Marie Jenney Howe, it met every Saturday in a Greenwich Village restaurant with the aim of bringing together women of unorthodox opinions for talk and comradeship. Its members (twenty-five to start, sixty by 1920) included Charlotte Perkins Gilman, the IWW organizer and orator Elizabeth Gurley Flynn, the wealthy radical socialite Mabel Dodge, the public health worker Dr. Josephine Baker, Gilman's disciple Henrietta Rodman, the socialists Rose Pastor Stokes and Katharine Anthony, the playwright Susan Glaspell, the journalist Rheta Dorr, the academics Leta Hollingsworth and Elsie Clews Parsons, the lawyer Crystal Eastman, the suffrage leaders Doris Stevens and Inez Milholland, and the Jungian psychoanalyst Beatrice Hinkle, along with the one African-American member, Grace Nail Johnson, a worker with the NAACP. Almost all were self-supporting and "unorthodox women"—according to Mabel Dodge, "women who did things and did them openly." The club meetings offered, as one said, to women who had "stepped out of their grooves" the "solidarity feeling" that trade unions offered workers and that "women so much lack."

In 1914 Marie Howe organized two public meetings at the Cooper Union to discuss "What Is Feminism?" The meetings drew a very large audience, though apparently with more men than women in attendance. The speakers included Clara Lemlich, who had called out the garment workers in 1909; the novelist Floyd Dell; the radical editor Max Eastman; and the future New Deal secretary of labor, Frances Perkins, still at this point a New York social worker. Notably the speakers broke out of the habit of emphasizing women's special moral qualities as entitling them to a wider field of action, and spoke forthrightly in terms of rights: the right to work, the right to vote, the right to unionize, and the right of mothers to work. In the same year, Heterodoxy member Henrietta Rodman, a New York schoolteacher, founded the Feminist Alliance, with the uncompromising individualist career-open-to-talents program of demanding "the removal of all social, political, economic, and other discriminations which are based upon sex, and the award of all rights and duties in all fields on the basis of individual capacity alone." She put her ideals into practice by launching a campaign to force the New York City school board both to employ married women and to offer maternity leave.

Conversation at the regular Heterodoxy meetings ranged over all the "causes" of the day. Sometimes guest speakers appeared, but on the most memorable occasions members were invited to talk about their own childhood and youth, or about how they were attempting to raise their own children in a free and modern way. Inez Haynes Irwin later recalled Heterodoxy as the place where the women "talked about everything." Rheta Dorr remembered things rather differently: "We thought we discussed the whole field, but we really discussed ourselves." To the new feminists, however, liberation entailed coming to terms with personal experience, from "growing up female" to passing on—or changing—the legacy in motherhood.

One idea the new feminists were in flight from was that of "Woman" itself, with all its moral freight of superior morality and purity. Whereas for the late-nineteenth-century woman's movement, "womanhood" had been both the glue of solidarity and the core of individual identity, to the feminists gender was but one attribute of personhood, in some situations primary, in most others irrelevant. "This morning," Parsons mused in her "Journal," "perhaps I may feel like a male; let me act like one. This afternoon I may feel like a female; let me act like one. At midday or at midnight, I may feel sexless; let me therefore act sexlessly." To her, "womanhood" was an available role that could be slipped on and off; personality transcended sex and gender. "The main objective of feminism, in fact," she wrote in her *Social Rule* (1916), "may be defeminization, the declassification of women as 'woman,' the recognition of women as human beings or personalities." This declassification was fundamental for liberation, since "the more thoroughly a woman is classified the more easily is she controlled."

One way that women were controlled was through their sexuality—by being regarded on the one hand as "the sex" (in the early-nineteenth-century usage) created purely for its sexual functions, and on the other as sex*less,* too pure to have strong sexual feelings. Much of the fight for women's rights and for a wider sphere so far had been based on the premise that women should be regarded as fully rounded human beings, not just "sex objects." By the early twentieth century, however, younger and well-educated women were beginning to wonder whether this downplaying of sex had not swung too far. Women were indeed human beings, but they were also sexual beings, and should not that sexuality be given full recognition and freedom? Like older women activists, they bitterly attacked the sexual "double standard"; but instead of insisting, like their mothers' generation, that men must be held to the same strict standards of sexual continence and fidelity as women, a few feminists were beginning to think that some degree of sexual latitude might be good for both sexes. Influenced by the new ideas of Freud, some indeed wondered whether it was partly the inhibition of women's sexuality that had also repressed their creativity and assertiveness in other realms. Certainly they were convinced that the closer comradeship of men and women they so desired depended on a greater frankness between the two, a breaking down of the Victorian constraints created by the supposed sexual innocence and "purity" of women.

In their greater willingness to acknowledge and explore sexuality, feminists might shock the more inhibited in the women's movement, but in fact they were but part of a wider cultural movement toward greater explicitness and publicity in sexual matters. It is difficult to know to what extent sexual practice was restrained in nineteenth-century America, but there were certainly well-defined limits as to what could be written or depicted in public. These were already expanding by the 1890s, and by the early twentieth century the proliferation of commercial urban pleasures directed mainly at the young working class, such as amusement parks, public dance halls, vaudeville, and the early movies, were offering greater opportunity for casual unchaperoned meeting and flirting between the sexes, together with increasingly frank erotic images and suggestions. As long as all this was confined to the working class, it could be seen as one of the pervasive social "problems" of the Progressive Era, requiring intelligent management and reform. Thus the policing of dance halls and the censoring of movies, and attempts to devise more wholesome recreations for young people. But once the new sexual openness appeared to be moving up to the middle class, it became a cultural revolution. A newspaper editor in 1913 could proclaim in a memorable phrase: It has struck "Sex O'Clock in America."

Many no doubt regretted, with the author of an *Atlantic Monthly* article of the following year, "the repeal of reticence," but it was a repeal that in fact owed a good deal to the activities of reformers bent on the more intelligent control of sexuality rather than its liberation. The WCTU and the women's movement in general tended to believe that sexual purity among youth could best be preserved by straightforward sex education rather than by ignorance. A considerable public scare about the growing incidence of venereal disease led medical reformers too to endorse sex education as part of a campaign of prevention. By 1920 about 40 percent of high schools offered some kind of sex education, and by 1921 medical examinations as a requirement for a marriage license had become standard in twenty states.

The continuing concern about prostitution, which became even more acute in the early twentieth century, led to open public discussions of this "social problem" in the press and periodicals. A number of cities followed the lead of Chicago in producing voluminous detailed reports on the vice trade. The same period also saw a public panic over the so-called white slave traffic, in which, purportedly, innocent young girls from the country, newly arrived in the city to find work, were lured, drugged, or kidnapped to a brothel and a life of shame. The press and magazines were filled with lurid stories about such incidents, some of which may have been true, and novels and movies followed. Women reformers stepped up their efforts to head off disaster by arranging for volunteers to meet young women at railway stations and steer them toward respectable lodgings, and in organizations like the YWCA offered recreation and housing to young female strangers in the city. Reformers argued that women police officers should be recruited and stationed in public places where women might be in danger of seduction.

The ritualistic stories that grew up around the notion of the white slave traffic performed a useful function. They mediated between the undoubted fact that urban prostitution was growing in numbers and profitability, and the cultural unwillingness to believe that a young woman would knowingly and of her own free will take up a life of paid sex. They also confirmed the cultural anxiety about the dangers to—and dangers of—the young woman outside the discipline of the family, when her own sexuality might become a trap for herself and then others. The various vice commission reports invariably linked prostitution to the growing numbers of young women who worked for wages in the cities. The wages were inadequate to live on, and yet the very fact that girls earned money, as the Massachusetts vice commission noted in 1914, "brings temptations, and makes them intolerant of restraint. It has become the custom of young women to go about freely, unaccompanied." It was not a woman's performance of labor that constituted the danger, but that she did so outside a family setting and received pay in return.

The "white slave" scare contributed to the passing in 1910 of the federal Mann Act, which made it a federal offense to transport women across state lines for "immoral purposes." The various official vice reports also led to temporarily effective crackdowns on red-light districts and the closing down of brothels. This certainly disrupted the vice trade, though it hardly eliminated prostitution. And all this reforming activity tended to paradoxical results. On the one hand, it increased fear of sexuality as essentially dangerous, particularly to women; on the other, it broke down the "conspiracy of silence" and opened up sexual questions to public scrutiny and debate to an unprecedented degree. By 1914, according to one comment, prostitution had become "a subject for polite conversation at the dinner table."

For feminists, however, sexual frankness was embedded not in the discourse of social problems but in a conscious commitment to female liberation and to the working out of freer and more honest relations between the sexes. Many feminists, like other cultural radicals, gravitated toward a major cultural phenomenon of the early twentieth century, the little "bohemias" of major cities, most especially New York's Greenwich Village, where low rents attracted artists, writers, political and social radicals, and hangers-on who liked the talk and the atmosphere. Although Greenwich Village was the most important and famous, by the turn of the century several American cities, including Chicago, had their little "bohemias." They were characterized by an unprecedented easy mixing of the sexes, and their infrastructure was maintained largely by women. It was women, reported one sociologist in the 1920s, who opened most of the studios, who "ran the tearooms and restaurants, most of the little art shops and books stalls, managed the exhibits and little theaters."

In New York after 1912 a major venue was the salon of Mabel Dodge, a wealthy and unconventional patron of advanced art and radical politics. Here could be found a heady mixture of radicals like the IWW leader Big Bill Haywood, the anarchist Emma Goldman, and self-consciously rebellious writers and artists. Most were socialists of one kind or another, but mainly they were committed to cultural revolution, the overthrow of Victorian repression, and personal liberation. The socialist revolution was desirable but rather a long way off; the quest for personal liberation was pressing and here and now. One of the major aims of Village bohemianism was to destroy feelings of shame about sex. Its adherents were convinced that the nineteenth-century double attitude toward women, in which they were both glorified and despised, made easy relations between the sexes impossible. The widespread ignorance about sex or even horror of it with which many brides began married life often got marriages off to a very rocky start. Mabel Dodge, herself continually in search of sexual fulfillment, made her salon a place where sex could be discussed frankly in mixed company.

The men as well as the women were feminists. Max Eastman, Crystal's brother, who edited the major vehicle of Village ideas, *The Masses*, founded the Men's League for Women Suffrage and made *The Masses* a vehicle for the discussion of feminism as well as socialism. The novelist Floyd Dell went so far as to claim that men were ultimately responsible for the women's movement, because men were changing their minds about what they wanted women to be—and women, as always, were responding to men's desires. "Men are tired of subservient women," he wrote in a series of newspaper articles in 1913, or rather they were tired of women who seemed to be demure and deferential but manipulated men to get their own way. "If only for self-protection," men now wanted "to find in woman a comrade and an equal." They were drawn to the new self-supporting, self-consciously liberated woman just because she "was comparatively freed from the home and its influence; because she took the shock and jostle of life's incident more bravely, more candidly and more lightly." The payoff of feminism for men was that it might free them from the burden of the conventional, feminine, dependent woman.

The intellectual gurus for a new sexual dispensation were the English writers Edward Carpenter and Havelock Ellis, and then Sigmund Freud. Carpenter's *Love's Coming of Age* (1896) and the multivolume *Studies in the Psychology of Sex* (1910–1928) by Ellis were soon available in the United States, and Freudian ideas became quickly assimilated into the cultural repertoire of American intellectuals after Freud lectured at Clark University in 1909. Carpenter preached a rather mystical gospel of free sexuality, including homosexuality. His essential message to women was that "every woman whose heart bleeds for the sufferings of her sex" should "hasten to declare herself *and to constitute herself as far as*

*she possibly can*, a free woman." Ellis was more scientific and
wrote frankly of the female orgasm. While insisting on sexual
pleasure as desirable in itself, quite apart from reproduction, he
also emphasized the differences between the sexes and thought
that motherhood was woman's supreme function. The gospel of
Freud, as received and interpreted by the young radicals, was
that the wellspring of personality and creativity lay in sexuality;
its repression led to sickness and neurosis.

A final intellectual influence on sexual discussion was the
Scandinavian Ellen Key, whose works were translated into English beginning in 1909 with her most famous work, *The Century
of the Child*, followed by *Love and Marriage* in 1911. Key considered herself a radical feminist, but her work, as many in the
women's movement recognized, showed the potential danger for
women of an exclusive focus on sex for liberation. Key's starting
point was the fundamental difference of men and women;
women, she thought, only misused their "woman power" by
competing with men and taking on men's jobs beyond the home
or agitating for the vote, which she considered worthless.
Woman had to make "the essence of her being the departure
point for her striving after liberation," and that essence was her
sexuality and above all her capacity for motherhood. This might
seem only a restating of Victorian truisms; indeed, Rheta Dorr
found Key's work both "old-fashioned" and "almost reac-
tionary." Yet she noted that "everybody who used to read Charlotte Perkins Gilman was now reading Ellen Key."

What made Key new and exciting was her insistence that
evolution demanded a new morality, in which sex expression, in
or outside marriage, was justified by love. Similarly a woman's
desire for a child was so basic to her nature that she was justified
in having one outside of wedlock. Key thus tried to break down
the taboos against single motherhood, just as she championed the
more respectable demand for state pensions for mothers, married
or not, because the mother deserved economic independence and
state support for her service to "the race."

Village women who were writers and artists often tried to combine marriage and motherhood with their careers. Village men and women were also committed, at least in theory, to marriages that were equal and open, repudiating possessiveness and ownership by either partner, and leaving each free to experiment with other sexual relationships. In practice most found that jealousy was a constant saboteur of these liberal convictions. For the women in particular, their principled commitment to nonpossessive and noncoercive relationships, their conviction that love should not compromise the freedom and self-development of either partner, meant that not only did they feel they had no right to demand fidelity from husbands or lovers, they did not even have the right to feel aggrieved when they did not get it.

Mabel Dodge wrote a rambling letter in 1913 to the novelist and fellow sufferer Neith Boyce about the problem of unfaithful partners, acknowledging that she felt she had no right to expect her younger lover, the journalist John Reed, to be faithful. "We are both individuals—we feel differently about this—that's all." But then she burst out: "This is so fundamental—is it what feminism is all about?" All women probably went through this, "but must they go on going thru it? Are we supposed to 'make' men do things? Are men to change? Is monogamy better than polygamy? Is it worse unhappiness to stay than to go? What do you think? . . . What is freedom anyway?"

Like many of the feminists of Heterodoxy, the radicals of Greenwich Village were searching for new habits of interaction between the sexes. They no longer wanted a relationship based on dominion and dependence, with its attendant behavior patterns of female coquetry and manipulation, but an easy comradeship of equals. They hoped that men and women could be lovers in a new way, but also that they could be friends. Max Eastman defined feminism as the belief in "breaking down sex barriers so that women and men can work and play and build the world together." Elsie Clews Parsons thought feminism was an expression of "the disappearing of fear between men and women."

Parsons herself was a strong exemplar of a woman who was unafraid, but she was quite aware of fear as a dominating thread in most women's lives: fear of men, fear of being alone, fear of flouting convention, of being perceived as unwomanly or unladylike. Parsons applied her anthropological approach to dissecting the lives of modern women, demonstrating that in the modern West, just as in more traditional or "backward" cultures, society controlled women through more or less elaborate systems of taboos and conventional constraints, which women themselves internalized and helped maintain.

Women might be defined as the class with a much more confined field of activity than men had. One of the minor but symbolically significant taboos that was being challenged in the early twentieth century was the taboo against women smoking. Now that we know so much about the perils of tobacco, it is difficult to realize what a symbol of liberation the cigarette once seemed. By the 1890s the occasional daring woman smoked in private; by 1905 so many women were lighting up that New York City passed an ordinance forbidding women to smoke in public. It was not smoking as such but smoking by *women* that was perceived as a transgressive act requiring public censure and prohibition, because smoking hitherto had been a distinctively male activity. Thus, to many people, smoking by women was perceived as indecent. To feminists, on the other hand, for men and women to smoke a companionable cigarette together was part of the effort to replace an acute sex awareness with the ease of comradeship. The young suffragist Florence Luscomb, visiting London, commented wistfully on the number of women she saw "so calmly smoking with the men. There was a human companionship about it that could almost make one imagine these men and women going amicably to the polls together."

Elsie Clews Parsons's own willingness to be adventurous, both physically and mentally, rested not only on her personality but on a comfortable cushion of money. She was the daughter of a wealthy and socially prominent family, educated at Barnard and with a Ph.D. from Columbia, and married to a rising Republican politician, Herbert Parsons. She continued her career as a writer and lecturer in anthropology at Columbia while bearing six children. In 1906 she wrote her first book, *The Family*, which she had intended as a textbook for college classes. But it aroused shocked reaction in the press for its advocacy of birth control and of "trial marriages" before couples had children and made a more permanent commitment. The *New York Herald* was particularly exercised that a woman in Elsie Parsons's social position should have published theories that "strike at the home and hence the State."

Parsons always maintained that while the state had a legitimate interest in parenthood, sexual relations in or out of marriage were purely private concerns. In *Fear and Conventionality* (1914) she looked forward to a society where "the impulses of sex will not be restricted in their expression to conjugality, nor will conjugality be considered as necessarily a habit for a lifetime." Her own marriage lasted until her husband's death, but during it both partners developed relations with others. Elsie had a number of male friends as well as lovers, and on anthropological field trips into the American Southwest had no qualms about traveling alone with a man. She was not alone in her sexual adventurousness. Inez Haynes Irwin always remembered a Heterodoxy member saying without embarrassment that she had lived with her husband a year before marriage in order to find out whether they were suited. "That was the first time I had ever heard any woman make a statement that, in my childhood and girlhood, would have been described as 'compromising.'" But the members of Heterodoxy were economically self-supporting, and therefore, Irwin realized, they could be "as independent of their own 'compromising' confessions as any man."

The breaking down of barriers between the sexes, which feminists were striving for so self-consciously, seems to some extent to have been occurring without the ideological freight in many areas of the wider culture. New venues and modes of heterosex-

ual sociability were emerging after 1900 that were acceptable to
the respectable middle classes. In new urban public spaces, belonging neither to work nor to the home—hotels with public
rooms, restaurants, cafés, nightclubs—the two sexes could mix,
mingle, and play without commitment. Most of the new dances
of the "dance craze" that swept the nation after 1910, like
the Turkey Trot, the Shimmy, and the Charleston, were bor-
rowed from working-class and particularly African-American
working-class culture, or from red-light districts like San Francisco's notorious Barbary Coast, though they were considerably
toned down for respectable middle-class consumption.

The changes taking place in relations between the sexes presented themselves most strikingly to contemporaries in the attitudes and appearance of the "girl." She appeared to present
herself to young men more as a "pal" than as a remote romantic
ideal, but at the same time she was also more overtly sexual than
the previous generation, and more frank in her language and
conversation. The columnist Dorothy Dix described the type of
girl attractive to men in 1915 as one who could play golf and
dance all night and drive a car and was not likely to swoon.
Older members of the women's movement were somewhat
stunned by the sudden nonideological assumption of freedom by
so many of the young. "I confess I am some times taken aback,"
admitted Jane Addams to the *Ladies Home Journal* in 1915, "at
the modern young woman; at the things she talks about and at
her free and easy ways."

By the 1910s new fashions in women's clothes were moving
away from the old corseted femininity, which emphasized hips
and bust, toward lighter, straighter, and looser dresses that dispensed with corsets but required naturally slim hips. The new
skimpier dresses and loss of petticoats were not only a blow to
the textile industry but a potential aesthetic disaster for the
middle-aged. By 1914 fashion commentators were sternly warn-
ing the older woman that "this is the day of the figure . . . the
body has to be as straight and yielding as every young girl's."

The new compulsion of the youthful silhouette was part of new emerging patterns of heterosexual sociability among the urban middle classes. In the nineteenth century, dancing had been for the young, but now middle-aged women were also learning the new dances, for the "tea dance" or nightclub was a place where a man might take his wife. Nineteenth-century customs in which sociability outside of courtship tended to take place among single-sex groups—men at the club or saloon, women at their club or sewing circle—were breaking down. The newer pattern seemed to be for men and women, including husbands and wives, to enjoy leisure activities together in mixed groups. Even the country clubs being built in the new outer suburbs billed themselves as places where husbands and wives could play golf or tennis together. Older women who kept up with the trends were now uneasily aware that it was no longer enough to be a good mother and a meticulous housekeeper; the modern wife was supposed to be a sparkling companion and lover to her husband as well. "In the old days a married woman was supposed to be a frump and a bore and a physical wreck," said one woman to Lydia Commander, only half jokingly. "Now you are supposed to keep up intellectually, to look young and well and be fresh and bright and entertaining."

By the early twentieth century the core ideal of marriage was moving away from the man and woman as parents to the couple as companions. The maintenance of that ideal would depend as much as anything on the ability to enjoy sex without the constant threat of pregnancy. In the long run the most significant development among the new attitudes toward sexuality was the movement to bring contraception and birth control out into the open as legal and indeed publicly endorsed practices. A freer attitude toward sex and a freer practice by women, plus the desire to pursue a career, or even to maintain a marriage in which companionship with a husband was more important than continual child-rearing and domesticity, all made contraception increasingly necessary. As Crystal Eastman said, birth control had to be a major component of the feminist struggle because "Feminists are not nuns." What was new, however, by the second decade of the twentieth century, was not the practice of contraception but its promotion as an articulate movement.

As the falling birthrate—so much decried by the mourners of "race suicide"—made clear, many married couples already practiced various forms of contraception. Still, after the 1873 "Comstock" laws, it was illegal to offer or disseminate information about contraceptive methods. A few states made an exception for medical colleges and books, but an official atmosphere of repression prevailed. The medical profession was divided over the desirability of contraception and the best methods, but in any case was unwilling to challenge the legal restrictions. The American Medical Association did not approve birth control as a legitimate aspect of medicine until 1937. At the same time condoms, which were regarded as preventatives against venereal disease rather than as contraceptives, were quite widely available, and it was possible to find various kinds of douches and pessaries—early diaphragms. Many couples relied on the so-called safe period, which unfortunately was not correctly understood at that time, or on periods of abstinence, or coitus interruptus. In the aggregate, combinations of these methods were clearly quite effective, but for the individual woman they were often hit or miss. And in order to use them women needed the cooperation of husbands, access to a sympathetic physician who would provide information or fit a pessary, or at least access to knowledgeable mothers, aunts, or female friends.

Lydia Commander found that among the upper classes some kind of contraceptive knowledge was "practically universal." She interviewed forty-six doctors in New York and found that all reported on being consulted about contraception. Most were willing to advise, though it was necessary to be careful. Among the many women she interviewed, she found that most wanted no more than two children, and that older women who had had large families were glad that their daughters were having smaller ones: "I never lived," said one, "but they do." Further down the social scale, however, such knowledge narrowed. Among the working class, especially the immigrant working class, families were traditionally much larger, and it was clear to reformers that the addition of one more child often meant the difference between continuing to get by and the slide into absolute poverty. Thus it was the working-class mother who suffered most. In the atmosphere of heightened sexuality in the early twentieth century, and in the face of the widespread practice of birth control and the use of contraceptives by the middle and upper classes, to ask the poor to exercise restraint seemed the height of bourgeois hypocrisy.

Bringing birth control out into the open drew on left-wing politics and its focus on the problems of the impoverished, and on feminist dedication to the liberation of women, as well as on new, more positive attitudes toward sexuality. A pioneer was Emma Goldman, a Russian-Jewish immigrant, midwife, anarchist, and fiery orator who toured the country preaching the gospel of a liberated female sexuality along with revolution. In 1910 she began to distribute pamphlets with explicit information on contraceptives. To her the exploitation of the working class, the quashing of political dissent, and the repression of sexuality were all part of the same capitalist authoritarian system, designed to grind out all joy and spontaneity in life in the service of the economic machine. Anarchism, she said, was not just a political theory but "a living influence to free us from inhibitions."

Freeing women from inhibitions was something the mainstream women's movement had not succeeded in doing, and according to Goldman, that was its biggest failure. In a 1906 essay, "The Tragedy of Women's Emancipation," she insisted that getting the vote or breaking into the professions was all very well, but they did not bring real emancipation as long as women were still enslaved to the "internal tyrants" of respectability and the fear of what other people would say. She was not much impressed by the modern emancipated woman, who she thought had become a "compulsory vestal," hobbled by the fear that love or motherhood would rob her of her hard-won freedom and independence. "How many emancipated women are brave enough to acknowledge that the voice of love is calling . . . ?" she demanded.

One of the people influenced by Goldman was a young wife and mother, Margaret Sanger. Sanger had grown up in an impoverished family, one of the eleven children of a stonecutter. She had also trained as a nurse, and even after her marriage and the birth of three children, she often worked as a nurse in obstetrics cases for Lillian Wald's Henry Street settlement in New York City. This brought her into contact with the poverty of the slums and the despair of poor women upon the arrival of one more child they had not known how to prevent. Sanger was struck with the ignorance that poor women seemed to have about their own bodies. Her husband was a socialist, and the couple were soon drawn into radical circles in Greenwich Village. At Mabel Dodge's salon, Sanger met Goldman, and also Big Bill Haywood and other left-wing socialists. She worked with the IWW in support of the great strike of textile workers in Lawrence, Massachusetts, in 1912, but she also began to write articles on sex education for the socialist newspaper *The Call*, entitled "What Every Girl Should Know." These did not deal directly with contraception, but they were explicit about sexual relations, and the Post Office decided it could not accept the newspaper for mailing because of the Comstock laws. The editors withheld her next article and left the space blank with the heading: "What Every Girl Should Know: NOTHING by order of the Post Office Department."

After a trip to Europe with her family, where she began to study European contraceptive methods, Sanger was ready to begin a public crusade for "birth control"—a term she coined. Birth control was necessary for women's sexual pleasure, for real companionship between husbands and wives, and for women's opportunity for a larger sphere of being. Women "can be nothing," wrote Sanger in her *Woman and the New Race* (1920), "as long as she is denied means of limiting her family." She situated birth control firmly in the context both of alleviating the often desperate economic and personal plight of poor women and of liberating women's sexuality. In this stage of her long career in the movement, she saw it as revolutionary rather than reformative, as freeing "the mind from sexual prejudice and taboo, by demanding the frankest and most unflinching reexamination of sex in its relation to human nature and the bases of human society." Mabel Dodge Luhan said of Sanger that she "was the first person I ever knew who was openly an ardent propagandist for the joys of the flesh."

Sanger began with a pamphlet, *Family Limitation*, which like Goldman's earlier effort was written in plain language and offered specific information on various kinds of contraceptives. To Sanger, birth control was always primarily a *woman's* issue, and so she was mainly interested in techniques to be used by women. Her experience among the poor had convinced her that cooperation by husbands could not be relied upon. Sanger tried to rally women out of their false modesty about contraception: they had to be prepared to take care of themselves and stop being squeamish and sentimental. It might seem "inartistic and sordid to insert a pessary or a suppository," she warned them, "but it is far more sordid to find yourself several years later burdened down with half-a-dozen unwanted children ... yourself a dragged out shadow of a woman." Finally, she urged readers of her pamphlet to teach other women what they had learned. IWW sympathizers printed up a hundred thousand copies and helped to distribute them.

Under threat of arrest, Sanger left for Europe again, even though World War I had already broken out. She visited birth-control clinics in Holland, where she learned about the latest contraceptive developments, and in London she met and was deeply influenced by Havelock Ellis. While she was in Europe, her husband was arrested in the United States for distributing

*Family Limitation.* But the publicity surrounding the pamphlet not only made Margaret Sanger famous, it led to the creation of a number of birth-control advocacy groups across the country. In New York a new National Birth Control League was founded by Mary Ware Dennett, an upper-class artist and divorced mother of two who for a while had been an NAWSA officer. The League attracted upper- and middle-class liberals and offered a new approach—not to flout the Comstock laws but to lobby governments for their repeal and so remove birth control from the legal definition of obscenity. Thus anyone would be able legally to disseminate information, and contraception would be lifted out of the category of "crime and indecency."

On her return to the United States, Sanger embarked on a triumphal speaking tour across the country, with much newspaper coverage and demonstrations both for and against her efforts. She was inundated by letters from women begging for her pamphlet. In July 1916 she decided to take direct action. With her sister, also a nurse, she opened a "birth control clinic" in a Jewish and Italian neighborhood of New York. The police soon closed it and arrested Sanger and her sister, who were sentenced to a month in jail. Across the country some twenty other birth controllers were arrested and faced varying jail sentences for giving out birth-control information. Among them was Emma Goldman, who gave a rousing speech to the court, reprinted in *The Masses*, proclaiming that birth control was essentially a "workingwoman's question," a battle in the "great modern social war" of the oppressed against capitalism and the state, "a war for a seat at the table of life."

Most of the thousands of letters that Sanger received came from working-class women, telling their stories and begging for help, but most of the people who joined the various birth-control leagues were middle-class, often professional men and women. The problem in turning birth control into a mass crusade was not creating a desire to use it but overcoming the reluctance to speak of it and be associated with it openly. A West Coast

IWW organizer wrote Sanger in 1915 that while she had found working-class women eager for contraceptive information, they also feared being associated with anything smacking of "immorality" and could not discuss their needs in public "without giggling and blushing." She suggested trained nurses who could work quietly among the neighborhoods, imparting the "secret" in confidential ways.

Even "advanced" women, who used birth control personally, were reluctant, as Mary Ware Dennett complained to her mother, "to come out in the *open* and help. Everyone is scared." In 1916, in support of Margaret Sanger, Elsie Parsons tried in vain to persuade twenty-five well-known women to testify openly that they had used contraceptives themselves. Parsons insisted that "public testimony on so private a matter . . . more than anything else would contribute to lift the taboo safeguarding the present law and the present practice of class discrimination. . . . At times, testimony about the private life takes on a sufficiently public significance to free it from ridicule or the charge of bad taste." But she found that the women could not bear the publicity, or felt that their husbands and children could not.

The question of birth control as a public movement widened the fissure between feminists and most of the mainstream suffrage movement. The suffrage leader Carrie Chapman Catt thought the issue was "sordid." "Free love," she replied to an appeal for endorsement from Sanger in 1914, "is not and never has been a tenet of suffragists. . . . If suffragists have a common aim along the line of morals it is toward self-control in private life, stricter laws for the control of public vice, and the enforcement of those laws." Even Charlotte Perkins Gilman, a member of Heterodoxy, was dubious. She was a radical, but of an older generation. Although she admitted the right of women to limit their families, she believed that the evolutionary purpose of sex was reproduction. When civilization had progressed to a higher level of development, she insisted, "we shall only crave this indulgence for a brief annual period, . . . and with no efforts at 'prevention,'

our average birth rate will be but two or three to a family."
Meanwhile she could not help but feel that "safe, free and unlim-
ited indulgence in the exercise" of sex was abnormal.

Sanger herself had worked briefly for the suffrage movement
in New York, but she thought it was absurd to postpone all other
change until the vote was won. In her autobiography she wrote
that "it seemed unbelievable" that suffrage leaders "could be serious in occupying themselves with what I regarded as trivialities
when mothers within a stone's throw of their meetings were
dying shocking deaths" from one more child too many. She
thought the suffragists' reluctance to come out for birth control
was due to their "inherited prejudices about sex . . . sex as such
was akin to sin, shame, and only the bearing of a child sanctioned
its expression."

Public, open acceptance of contraception would mean accepting the decisive severance of sex from reproduction. It would
mean social acceptance of sexuality as something to be enjoyed
for its own sake, as much by women as by men. But what would
be the consequences of this revolutionary disjuncture? The
nineteenth-century advocates of the women's movement had always publicly defended the cause of what they called "voluntary
motherhood," by which they meant a wife's right to decide when
she would become a mother, and thus her right to refuse her husband's sexual advances. This claim to "self-ownership" was in
fact a radical challenge to the traditional religious and legal claim
of a husband to his wife's body in marriage. Few women in the
women's movement had any religious objection to artificial contraception, but they saw birth control as part of the sexualization
of the social atmosphere, the redefinition of women as primarily
sex objects that the movement had been dedicated to escaping.
Many of the older activists feared that once apprehension of
pregnancy was removed, women would have no effective argument to deter the constant sexual demands of men. As Elsie
Clews Parsons had pointed out (approvingly) in her controversial
1906 book on the family, with improvements in contraception

"the need for sexual restraint as we understand it may disappear." For many women this was exactly the problem.

One might argue that the availability of effective birth control has been responsible for the most profound change in women's condition in the twentieth century. But it remained a cause of the dedicated few, though increasingly used by the anonymous many. Unlike the vote, birth control was not the occasion for mass marches down Fifth Avenue, and it coexisted uneasily not only with the suffrage organizations but also with much of the broader women's movement. Fundamental to women's liberation though it was, it remained a stand-alone crusade.

# 5

# War and Victory

To me the ballot is in a Republican democracy the signer of absolute equality.—Angelina Weld Grimké, 1918

The right of citizens of the United States to vote shall not be denied or abridged by the United States or by any state on account of sex.—Nineteenth Amendment, 1920

ACCORDING TO Rheta Dorr, "Woman Suffrage in America began to wake up from its long lethargy in 1907–8." Younger suffragists who thought of themselves as insurgents probably exaggerated the "lethargy" of the movement in the first few years of the century, but by the second decade it did seem to take off. Susan Anthony had handpicked her successor, choosing the forty-one-year-old Iowan Carrie Chapman Catt, who had proved her mettle as an organizer in the successful Colorado campaign. Catt was a college graduate and had been a school-teacher before her marriage. In 1904, when her husband became seriously ill, she resigned from the presidency of the NAWSA in order to nurse him, and then spent the next several years as a leader of the International Woman Suffrage Alliance, founded that year. The unmarried Anna Howard Shaw, who was an M.D., a licensed Methodist preacher, and a professional lecturer,

succeeded her. Shaw was by all accounts an inspiring and popular speaker, but she was not a good administrator, and the
NAWSA suffered under her rather inefficient leadership. In
1915 Catt, now widowed, again became president, and it was she
who was at the helm for the ultimate victory campaign in 1919.
To get to that point required the invigoration of new ideas, people, and tactics.

After the victories of the 1890s, no further states were added
to the suffrage camp until 1910. Suffragists later dubbed this
period the "doldrums," when the movement seemed to be be-
calmed and nothing important was happening. Recently historians have begun to appreciate that this was a period in which the
suffrage organization began to rethink its strategies, making significant attempts to reach out to new segments of the female
population. While by the end of the century every state had some
kind of suffrage organization and clubs, many were largely inac-
tive, and membership tended to fade away once the excitement
of a state campaign or visits by prominent national suffrage figures had passed. By 1900 the dues-paying membership of the
NAWSA was no more than nine thousand, and its class and ethnic range was both narrow and aging. It was also chronically
short of funds. Suffrage women tended to come from the old
Protestant native-born middle class of small business and professionals—they were economically comfortable but did not have
much cash to spare. Devotion to the "Cause," as they had come
reverently to call the suffrage movement, had become a habit
rather than an urgent militancy.

Nor, apart from the WCTU, had the NAWSA been able to
make strategic alliances with the pillars of "organized womanhood," such as the General Federation of Women's Clubs. Indeed, the many new associations that were attracting women at
the turn of the century, organizing their energies and channeling
them into new public activities beyond the home, were rivals
for the allegiance of "restless" women. Women were on the
move, but suffragists had not been able to make themselves the

leaders and shapers of that movement. Younger leaders were re-
alizing that if the movement was not to disappear entirely, it
needed to greatly expand its membership, become somewhat
more inclusive, and attract younger women; it needed to stream-
line its strategies and organization; it needed to attract more
press attention; it desperately needed to raise funds; and it
needed some excitement and glamour.

In her brief first tenure as NAWSA president, Catt had inau-
gurated a deliberate "society" plan to recruit well-to-do-elite
women. In the successful Colorado campaign she and Lucy
Stone had successfully brought the elite women of Denver to declare openly for suffrage and noted how respectful this seemed to
make press coverage. During an unsuccessful campaign in 1894,
when New York State was revising its constitution, suffragists
were surprised to find themselves aided by a number of "women
of social influence" in New York City who had never previously
shown any public interest in the suffrage question. Led by the
prominent doctor Mary Putnam Jacobi and Mrs. Josephine Shaw
Lowell, the aristocratic leader of charity organizations, they set
up headquarters in Sherry's, a fashionable restaurant, and secured numerous signatures for a suffrage petition.

This was the beginning of a steady stream of the wealthy and
fashionable into the suffrage movement. Anna Howard Shaw's
great coup was to attract the fabulously wealthy Alva Belmont,
who had already signaled her willingness to be unconventional
by divorcing her first husband. Belmont was an imperious
woman whose bad treatment of her servants was notorious, but
she was genuinely devoted to the cause, and her money was gen-
erously given to support striking working women as well as suffrage propaganda. Other well-to-do and prominent women
converts included Katherine Mackay, wife of the founder of the
International Telephone and Telegraph Company, Mrs. William
Vanderbilt, and the wealthy art collector Louisine Havemeyer.

The adherence of such women, coupled with greatly enhanced fund-raising efforts, brought in much needed money for

the movement. Many suffrage societies could now pay their office and field workers, and the NAWSA was able to step up its educational campaigns, distribute suffrage literature to high schools and libraries, and sponsor debates and essay competitions. It could also afford to move its headquarters in late 1909 from the backwater of Warren, Ohio, to New York City. The support of fashionable women also ensured more favorable attention from the press, and their patronage gave the movement a social imprimatur that made it easier for many more timid middle-class women to join. A number of well-known actresses, including the celebrated beauty Lillian Russell, the young Ethel Barrymore, and the movie star Mary Pickford, also came out for suffrage, adding glamour to the cause.

Professional women had generally felt that the only way to succeed in their careers was to keep their heads down, concentrate on excelling at their work, and stay out of controversial political movements. By 1910, however, many professional women were coming to realize their marginal status and lack of real equality, and this helped to pull many toward suffrage. As women in the reform communities became more involved with government and turned increasingly to the state for aid, they became more visible and effective advocates for suffrage.

The NAWSA leadership recognized the age-profile of its membership as a problem. The women's movement had never been a movement of the young. The pioneers of the 1850s had been in their thirties or above, usually married and with children, and most activists into the twentieth century were solidly middle-aged. Susan Anthony retained control of the NAWSA until she was eighty; Carrie Chapman Catt was fifty-six when she became president of the organization for the second time and led the final push for victory. The dominance of mature women in the movement was partly a function of the longevity of the struggle, so that activists grew old along with it. It was also partly due to the fact that the secondary and subordinate place of women in the world did not really hit home to most women until their girlhood was over. The freedom and indulgence allowed the "American girl," in contrast to European girls, was something on which all commentators on American life, from Alexis de Tocqueville to Henry James, remarked. As Rheta Dorr remembered small-town life in the 1880s, "all its social life centered around and was dominated by the ephemeral young lady," though when she married, "she sank without trace."

By the turn of the century, girls with ambitions beyond the social were finding higher education and new kinds of work opening up to them. Perceiving themselves on a cresting wave of opportunity, most felt no need to attach themselves to an organized women's movement. Perhaps most important, the young woman was still negotiating her relations with the opposite sex, and was either exultant at her newfound sexual power over men, or in despair if she appeared to lack it. In either case, she would be reluctant to enlist in a movement of middle-aged women who had acquired the reputation of being "anti-male." As one feminist sympathizer, whose mother had been a suffragist, explained her own early lack of active involvement: she wanted to get married, and "girls who were trying to get married at that time didn't shout their heads off about woman's suffrage, as yet not very popular with men."

Young women, even more than their mothers, were easily spooked by adverse public opinion and ridicule. Nora Stanton Blatch decided to form a suffrage club at Cornell where she was studying engineering, and managed to recruit sixteen coeds. But when their first meeting was prominently reported in the *Cornell Sun*, with an editorial attack "painting the women members as disturbed human beings," most of them immediately resigned, including the two daughters of the president of the New York State Woman's Suffrage Association. It took their mother's prompt descent on campus to stiffen her daughters' backbones. But two Radcliffe students, Maud Wood Park and Inez Haynes Gilmore (Irwin), both of whom later became important suffragists, organized a College Equal Suffrage League, and by 1912 there was a National College Equal Suffrage League with chapters on many campuses and a circulating library of books and pamphlets. From 1906 NAWSA leaders began a concerted effort to recruit college students, and college events at conventions became a staple.

At the same time the NAWSA's membership was growing, new leaders were emerging who were prepared to take more aggressive directions. One of the most important was Harriot Stanton Blatch, the daughter of Elizabeth Cady Stanton, who returned to the United States in 1902 after twenty-two years in Britain, where she had married a well-to-do businessman. There she had been involved with Fabian socialism and the labor movement, and on her return to the United States she quickly joined the New York branch of the WTUL.

Born in 1856, Blatch was a transitional figure; like her mother, but unlike her own daughter Nora, she had never had to earn her own living. Still, like her mother, she saw the value of economic independence, what Elizabeth Stanton had dubbed "the peculiar sacredness of the individual check book"; and like the younger feminists born in the 1870s and 1880s, she identified paid work as the major vehicle of women's emancipation. She was convinced that the economically independent woman was also the key to winning suffrage at last, because "the woman who supports herself has a claim upon the state." In 1907 she founded the Equality League of Self-Supporting Women, which was open to any woman who worked for a living, professionals and blue-collar workers alike. The name is significant, showcasing both the demand for a global "equality," which was increasingly glossed over in standard suffrage rhetoric, and its members' primary self-identification as their "independence." Its inclusive membership policy reflected a rather naive belief that the experience of paid work itself, no matter what kind, joined all female earners into a new cohesive class.

By 1908 the Equality League had twenty thousand members ranging from trade-union women to reformers such as the nursing pioneer Lavinia Dock and Greenwich Village radicals such as Inez Milholland. Blatch also brought in Leonora O'Reilly and Rose Schneiderman from the WUTL, and organized a group of New York blue-collar working women to testify at state suffrage hearings in Albany. In the aftermath of the 1910 shirtwaist strike, Blatch became estranged from the New York WUTL and reformulated the Equality League into the Women's Political Union. The organization now focused exclusively on the intensive lobbying of politicians. Like Susan Anthony and Carrie Chapman Catt, Blatch had also decided that success in getting the vote demanded absolute concentration on that issue alone, and that allies ought to be selected with that in mind. Wealthy women with political connections were more useful in this context than working-class women.

Nonetheless, under the influence of women like Blatch and the suffragists in the WUTL, movement leaders began to make a stronger effort to reach out to wage-earning women. Some state suffrage societies were more committed to working-class interests than others. The Illinois State Woman Suffrage party declared proudly in 1911 that it was the first to link suffrage with "women's industrial betterment" as part of the keystone of its constitution. Whereas the "older suffragists" fought shy of "entangling alliances" with other issues, "the new generation boldly assume suffrage as a means to an end, valuable only as related to that end in the mind of every suffragist." The "older suffragists" of the NAWSA saw a more pragmatic utility in working-class adherents, as speakers to appeal to workingmen and lobby legislators with labor ties. The organization hired Rose Schneiderman in 1912, for example, to work as an organizer among working people in an unsuccessful Ohio suffrage campaign, and Clara Lemlich, who had soared to fame for her role in the garment workers' strikes, became one of their paid workers in New York. The relationship was not without strain. Working-class women often felt uncomfortable at NAWSA meetings, feeling either patronized or ignored, and with the new visibility of the very wealthy in NAWSA ranks this feeling increased. The president of the California Wage Earners Suffrage League told the middle-class members of the state suffrage convention tartly that they "had no conception of the meaning of the word wage-earning."

Distrust of middle- and upper-class suffragists, however, did not necessarily deter working women from the pursuit of suffrage itself. As both middle-class women interested in labor and working women themselves sought to gain various kinds of protective legislation, rather than rely on trade-union organizing, the ability to vote seemed more salient and necessary. All women ought to have the vote, declared Leonora O'Reilly of the WUTL to a Senate committee on woman suffrage, "but we working women must have it."

The situation was much the same for organized African-American women. With much cause, they too came to distrust the mainstream suffrage movement but also strongly supported suffrage. By the twentieth century a growing number of African-American women were both well educated and self-supporting, and saw full citizenship as their right. For African Americans too, suffrage had a particular poignancy and immediacy because black men in the South had briefly enjoyed the right to vote after the Civil War and had then been effectively disfranchised. The National Association of Colored Women (NACW) included among its leaders several strong suffragists: Josephine S. Pierre Ruffin of Boston; Mary Church Terrell, a teacher from Washington, D.C. (the first president); Ida B. Wells Barnett; the teacher Margaret Murray Washington, the wife of Booker T. Washington; and Mary McCurdy, a temperance leader from Georgia. These women were striving to defend and protect their race as well as assert their rights as women, and they were quite ready to challenge white suffragists.

The white leadership, on the other hand, was determined to keep the entire race question out of the movement, calculating that it could only lead to trouble. Any move that seemed to hint

at racial inclusiveness might prompt Southern members to se-
cede; on the other hand, most of the NAWSA's non-Southern
membership was unwilling to follow the Southern lead into an
unequivocal endorsement of discrimination, and was uncomfortable with forthright racist language.

Even so, African-American women were constantly rebuffed
when they endeavored to join the mainstream movement. Some
state branches of the NAWSA in the North and West included
black women in their associations, and a number of white suffragists as *individuals* were involved with movements for racial justice. Mary White Ovington, the white head resident at a New
York settlement house, was one of the founders of the National
Association for the Advancement of Colored People (NAACP)
in 1908, and Jane Addams was a member. Most white suffragists,
however, even those who deplored the often virulent racism of
the period, could not see issues of racial discrimination as primary, and they could not make the connection between racism
and sexism that had been possible, at least sometimes, to the pioneers like Stanton. At the 1909 NAWSA convention, Carrie
Chapman Catt had tried to deflect the blatant white supremacist
arguments of Mississippian Belle Kearney, pleading, "Let us try
to get nearer together and to understand each other's ideas on the
race question and solve it together." Of course she meant that
Northern and Southern *whites* should learn to understand each
other's position; understanding the race question did not mean
consultation with African Americans. If getting the vote was the
most important aim, racial issues had somehow to be finessed.

African-American women appreciated the essential kinship of
racism and sexism. In 1911 at the NAWSA convention in
Louisville, an African-American delegate tried to persuade the
organization to recognize this kinship, attempting to introduce a
resolution "that it is as unjust and undemocratic to disfranchise
human beings on the ground of color as on the ground of sex."
The executive, led by Anna Howard Shaw, rejected the pro-

posed resolution as "unsuitable," largely because it seemed to be a breach of genteel good manners to introduce a statement that would "do nothing but create discord and inharmony," to the discomfort of their Southern white hosts. Throughout the period the NAWSA continued to deny the requests of black groups for delegate status at national conventions. When suffrage marches became a regular part of campaigns after 1908, African-American women who wanted to march were usually required to do so as a separate contingent at the back of the parade.

Race remained a constant challenge for the suffragists right through to the final victory in 1920. Once the NAWSA decided to revive the campaign for a constitutional amendment in 1915, Catt was convinced that support from a few Southern states would be crucial both for getting the measure through Congress and then for ratification. The NAWSA therefore could not afford to be associated with anything that might smack of breaking down the color line. On the other hand, in the Northern and Western states black men voted, and as more states adopted woman suffrage, so did black women. Forty-five percent of the 1,373 African-American voters in Denver in a 1906 election were women, and one commentator reckoned that a proportionately larger number of black women voted than white. In 1917, when New York enacted woman suffrage, 75,000 African-American women registered to vote. The formation of the NAACP in 1909 and the Urban League a year later signaled that an organized body of African Americans was prepared to mount a strong, articulate challenge to racial discrimination.

W. E. B. Du Bois, the prominent spokesman for black civil rights, was a strong supporter of woman suffrage—though he had few illusions about the commitment of white suffragists to the rights of black women—and his magazine *The Crisis* often printed articles on the subject. By 1917 Carrie Chapman Catt was writing in *The Crisis* and assuring its readers that the NAWSA stood for equal rights for all, even while trying to keep

her Southern wing in tow by assuring *them* that the formal removal of sex as a barrier to voting would not undermine the particular arrangements each state might make to regulate voting
eligibility.

Developments abroad also pushed the suffrage movement in
new directions. American suffragists had led the way in creating
an international women's suffrage movement, but while the pace
of enfranchisement stalled in the United States, women won the
vote in New Zealand in 1893, Australia in 1902, and Finland in
1906. These were, to be sure, small and "peripheral" countries,
but in 1912 during the Chinese revolution, for a brief period the
women of Nanking Province were also enfranchised. Feeling
themselves part of a worldwide "rising" of women buoyed suffragist spirits in the United States, while chagrin at being over-
taken in modernity by other countries provided a useful
propaganda tool. During the California suffrage campaign of
1911, the organizers found a group of Australian boys whom
they hired to parade with banners reading "Our mothers can
vote, why can't yours?" And in New York in 1912 Anna
Howard Shaw herself carried a banner declaring "Catching up
with China!"

The most important influence from abroad came from
Britain. The British women's suffrage movement had begun
later than the American and owed much to its example and influence; for a long time it had seemed more cautious and conservative. By 1907, however, the British movement was being
galvanized into a new militancy by Blatch's old friend Emmeline
Pankhurst and her daughters. The Pankhursts introduced tactics
adopted from the labor and the Irish independence movements:
open-air street-corner speaking, dramatic processions, and, most
controversial, civil disobedience. A number of American women
activists had spent time in Britain and had been involved in these
new developments, and in any case they were well reported in
the American press. Yet somehow the cloak of respectability
hung rather more heavily upon American suffragists than on

their British counterparts, so most older American suffragists were initially quite dubious about marches and speaking on street corners—these were the tactics of strikers, anarchists, and agitators. And the Americans were appalled when some British suffragettes started a wave of window breaking and other symbolic destruction of property. Having spent decades building a picture of the potential woman voter as a paragon of sober morality and civic duty, American suffragists saw this lawless image from abroad as no more than deadly ammunition for their opponents.

Blatch, however, and many of the younger women were convinced that adopting the nonviolent aspect of these British tactics was just what was needed to jolt the American movement into life again. Apart from its annual conventions, the NAWSA's cautious approach had been to meet women on their home ground where they were most comfortable, in churches and church halls, and above all in "parlor" meetings, where small groups would be gathered together in someone's home to receive a little gentle suffrage propaganda along with tea and cakes. Blatch decided that suffrage had to come out of the parlor.

The first British suffrage march had occurred in 1907; the Americans were not far behind with a small New York City parade organized by Blatch in 1908, another in California, and one in Boone, Iowa, the same year. Mary Jane Coggeshall, honorary president of the Iowa Women's Suffrage Society, marched at the head of its parade with great trepidation: "It wasn't so bad after all," she acknowledged afterward. By 1911 parades were larger and better orchestrated. Ten thousand people, according to the *New York Times*, which devoted a special section to the event, marched up Fifth Avenue in New York in 1912 in an evening parade led by fifty women on horseback. Many of the marchers were organized into contingents identified by occupation: nurses, teachers, social workers, college students; there was also a "colored women's division." Several society women were conspicuous, including Alva Belmont who joined in leading a delegation of factory workers. Large and respectful crowds watched, and the spectacle convinced the apprehensive *Times* that women would very likely get the vote unless men were "firm and wise enough" and "masculine enough to prevent them."

Thereafter the suffrage parade became a fixture of the movement. For women to march was a defiant tactic, for it meant they were appropriating a mode of behavior associated with working-men—like the great Labor Day parades, or marches by strikers, or the giant parades of political parties, though these were now in decline. Above all, the parades, along with all the other new methods that suffragists began to adopt, like plays, skits, and even suffrage movies, were making suffrage more fun. Organizing them and taking part was much more enjoyable than the usual dogged suffrage work.

These new activities also cost much more money than the old church hall and parlor meetings, and made it more important to attract upper-class women with ready checkbooks. In 1914 Carrie Chapman Catt received an unexpected bequest from the late Mrs. Frank Leslie (a publishing widow) to employ for the cause of woman suffrage, and she used it to publish and distribute a massive amount of suffrage propaganda.

Open-air speaking on street corners or at factory gates was another new tactic that many older suffragists found either frightening or unladylike. But younger suffragists came to relish it, learning to be brief and to the point, to deal with hecklers and retort with a snappy answer, and to maintain good humor. Younger suffrage organizers were also much more attuned than the older members to the new commercial culture of the twentieth century, and they easily adopted many of the techniques of modern advertising. They placed large billboards at city intersections and advertisements on streetcars; they persuaded city store owners to display suffragist colors—yellow, white, and purple—in their windows. Rose O'Neill, creator of the popular Kewpie doll, was a staunch suffragist, and she drew Kewpie postcards for the NAWSA to sell. From the established political parties, suffragists adopted the idea of suffrage "buttons" and pins as an easy way for women to show a public commitment. Supporters were urged to wear their pins in public to bring suffrage to the notice of others and solidify the loyalty of the wearer herself.

Suffrage pins were soon followed by suffrage sashes, hats, and even blouses. In New York the NAWSA appointed Macy's as its "official" purveyor of suffrage paraphernalia. Business soon came to perceive the commercial possibilities in suffrage. Chambers of commerce solicited the NAWSA and its local branches to bring their conventions to their town; big stores decorated their windows with suffrage colors when a parade was to pass by. Mary Ware Dennett in 1911 remarked on a large advertisement she had noticed in a streetcar, for soap or something like it, proclaiming that "All women vote for ——": it wouldn't have been there, she insisted, "if it didn't pay to have it there, and it couldn't have used those words if the suffrage movement had not become an asset to the commercial world." Plenty of people still ridiculed the idea of women voting, but when commerce began to pay respectful attention, it was surely a sign that the eventual triumph of woman suffrage could not be far off.

Another crowd-pleasing innovation was the use of the new automobile. Motoring in the new open-top cars was dusty and not particularly comfortable, but women who could afford it quickly took to the charms of motoring, and many learned to drive. Some suffragists early appreciated the possibilities of the automobile for propaganda tours. "We must seek on the highways the unconverted," declared Harriot Stanton Blatch, and indeed the appeal of the vehicle, if not the message, could be relied on to draw an interested crowd of men wherever the cavalcade stopped for speeches. The most eloquent message, however, was probably the subliminal one: the sight of a woman at the wheel, demonstrating both the new freedom and the new competence of her sex.

The motoring, the marches, the outdoor speeches, the general color and élan of the new campaigns were making suffrage front-page news that could not be ignored. As early as 1910 Inez Haynes Irwin could write to her old college friend Maud Park that suffrage "is actually fashionable now. . . . The movement which when we got into it had about as much energy as a dying kitten, is now a big, virile, threatening, wonderful thing." In 1916 the NAWSA claimed 100,000 members and for the first time surpassed the membership of the WCTU.

Besides making suffrage more visible and modern, the move out of the parlors and church halls into the open air was part of a shift in the movement's target audience. The message of the women's movement had always been directed primarily at women themselves, urging them to turn their vague discontents and personal grievances into more constructive channels of self-assertion and self-development. The vote, however, was a legal right that had to be wrested from *men*; they were the gatekeepers who held political power. While the new and more colorful methods appealed to younger women who responded to the excitement and the fun, the soapbox speeches and parades also spoke directly to the male voter where he was likely to be found: at the factory gates and on the streets.

The women's movement had always enjoyed a number of male allies. At least five hundred men marched in the 1912 New York parade, and on college campuses men's groups for women's suffrage had begun to appear. Max Eastman founded the Men's League for Woman Suffrage, which by 1912 had become an international organization. Many suffragists remarked that on their speaking tours they often found men more responsive than women. Florence Luscomb, one of the new young suffragists, thought the parades had been useful in winning over men because "it gave them visual proof that women who wanted the suffrage were ordinary representative women . . . and not the unsexed freaks the anti's declared they were."

Recognition of political realities was also modifying and expanding suffrage arguments. At the turn of the century it was common for suffragists to blame immigrant voters for their

many defeats and to express bitter resentment that recent immigrant men, who in many states were allowed to vote before taking out formal citizenship, and "ignorant" African-American
men could vote while native-born educated white women could
not. This resentment seems to have been a powerful motive in
bringing many native-born women to suffrage and was by no
means restricted to elite women. The wife of a postal worker,
Maria Farnsworth, exulted the day after women won the suffrage in Kansas in 1912 that now "My vote counts as much as any
negro's—as any dago's."

In the South suffragists made the argument that giving votes
to white women would strengthen white supremacy, and in the
rest of the country that it would bolster the political position
of Americans of "Anglo-Saxon" stock against hordes of newcomers. In adopting the language of Anglo-Saxon superiority,
old-stock white women could co-opt for themselves the assumption of racial superiority of their men while glossing over sex inferiority. By the early twentieth century, however, many suffrage
leaders were beginning to realize that this approach was counterproductive. After all, a fair proportion of the male electorate, especially in the Eastern states, was non-Anglo-Saxon. However
much they might personally resent the "ignorant foreign vote,"
suffragists would have to tone down their rhetoric about ignorant foreigners in order to win a sufficient number of voters at
the polls.

In addition, as the movement expanded its working-woman
membership it was also automatically expanding its ethnic basis,
since such a large proportion of urban working women were immigrants or of immigrant parentage. Yet when immigrant
women became interested in suffrage they were more likely to
join separate "wage-earner" suffrage leagues rather than the
NAWSA. Often too, they were more readily influenced by suffrage developments in their countries of origin than by NAWSA
propaganda. The revolution in Nanking in 1912 stimulated
more Chinese women on the West Coast to support suffrage

than any actions of the American movement. Even though it learned to print its pamphlets in numerous languages when campaigning in big cities, the NAWSA never developed a concerted effort to appeal to or work with ethnic communities. Basically it continued to think of them as unmovable enemies of women's emancipation, rather than as potential allies to be won over.

Most "ethnic" men, like most native-born men, resisted the idea of woman suffrage, but there was considerable variation in the degree of hostility. Irish voters tended to be the most unfriendly—even though there were many Irish women active in labor organizing—followed by German and Italian men. The Jewish communities in Eastern cities, which had a strong radical complexion, tended to be favorable, as did Scandinavians and Finns. In the 1917 successful referendum in New York, for example, the Jewish wards of the city voted a strong "yes." For suffragists, the problem was not just the ethnic vote itself but its impact on native-born voters. The specter of increasing the immigrant vote by the enfranchisement of immigrant women was enough to deter many old-stock voters and even some women who might otherwise have been favorably disposed to suffrage. It was bad enough having "Paddy" as a voter, complained the novelist Margaret Deland; was it necessary to have "Bridget too"?

If the suffrage movement remained largely old stock in personnel, and suffragists never became comfortable with the fact of ethnic diversity in America, they did come to realize that people approached the question of the vote with different interests and aims, and they were learning to tailor their arguments to their audience. For example, the cultural belief in women's moral superiority could be usefully called upon to appeal to upper-class men and women concerned with corruption in government: women would sweep out the Tammany Hall–type city bosses and bring in honest men. To those concerned with vice, suffragists emphasized women's interest in temperance and their determination to stamp out prostitution; to working women they pointed out that they needed to vote to protect themselves from sweated labor and exploitative employers; to mothers, they recalled their duty to help shape the wider world in which their children would grow up. To the growing community of social workers and progressives, they insisted that government would fully recognize its responsibility for social justice only when women were accorded full citizenship. The most ubiquitous and probably most successful argument was the assertion that since much of local government was simply housekeeping writ large, the housekeepers of the country had both the right and the duty to bring their natural skills to bear upon its administration. The effectiveness of this idea showed up in the many political cartoons—one of the most long-lived of political images—of the woman with a broom sweeping out corruption and inefficiency from the political household.

At the same time mainstream suffragists realized they would have to quiet fears that women's suffrage might somehow have disrupting effects on the social order or its bedrock, the family. They endeavored to portray it rather as a natural evolutionary development of the modern world, a mark of progress, not revolution. Women's suffrage, the working woman Caroline Lowe explained to a Senate committee, offered the legislators "a glorious opportunity to place yourselves abreast of the current of this great evolutionary movement," to take "your places as men of affairs in the world's progress."

Older arguments about women's natural *right* to participate in government through the vote, or as recognition of the natural *equality* of women with men, did not entirely disappear, but they were certainly subordinated to an insistence on the practical benefits that the vote would confer on women, and that the woman voter would in turn confer on the country. Aileen Kraditor, in a highly influential 1965 formulation, wrote that the women's movement in the early twentieth century shifted from arguments from justice to arguments from expediency. It would be fairer to say that the suffragists' arguments changed to match the changing function of politics itself.

Before the turn of the century, apart from war, government rested very lightly on white Americans. When it touched people directly it was usually as a dispenser of patronage and jobs. Electoral politics, however, were matters of high enthusiasm among the male electorate. Voter turnout reached an all-time high in the 1880s to 1890s, and party identification was strong. Political conventions and great political torchlight parades were major demonstrations of popular enthusiasm, in which men signified their masculine identity as equal participants in the republic and their loyalty to the party. By the twentieth century, however, the nature of politics was changing: party loyalty was slipping and with it the enthusiasm and turnout of male voters. At the same time political battles began to have more positive content, and many different groups of people engaged in politics with specific agendas. The vote, inevitably, was transformed from a demonstration of equal citizenship into a weapon for specific policy ends.

By 1910 the suffrage cause was being swept up by the general political movement of progressivism. As women reformers and civic improvers among the progressives became frustrated at their slow progress and lack of leverage as nonvoters, they began to see the importance of suffrage. Male progressives also saw the woman voter as a natural ally for reform, whether in cleaning up corruption in government or mitigating the worst social effects of unregulated capitalism. Meanwhile those progressives who pressed for greater direct popular involvement in politics through such procedural innovations as the initiative, referendum, and recall raised the issue of how democracy could be implemented and therefore of those who were excluded from it.

The first great twentieth-century breakthrough for suffrage came in the California campaign of 1911, which demonstrated the importance of progressivism for success. There had already been a surprise victory in Washington State the year before, but California was electorally more populous and important. In 1910 progressives controlled the state government and approved a referendum for a woman suffrage amendment in the 1911 election. By that time not only the twenty thousand members of the Federation of Women's Clubs but the State Nurses Association, the Mother's Congress, the Native Daughters of the Golden West, the Catholic Ladies Aid Society, women's labor unions, associations of collegiate alumnae, and African-American clubwomen were all on board and ready to apply pressure, demonstrate, and organize to persuade male voters. The Socialist party was also a particularly effective ally in the California campaign.

A strong strain of native socialism could be found in the United States by the turn of the century, especially in the Midwest and Far West, with roots in the Social Gospel, Christian socialism, and Bellamyite nationalism. Socialists of this type were sympathetic to women's suffrage and often staunch workers for it. Even the Marxist-inspired Socialist Party of America, founded in 1901, which had usually regarded the women's movement as essentially bourgeois and a distraction from the major problem of the class struggle, by 1908 seemed to be waking up to the woman question. Socialists' new attention was signaled by the designation of the last Sunday in February 1909 as Woman's Day; this soon became a permanent fixture on the socialist calendar and by 1915 was marked by mass spectacles in major cities. Socialist women themselves were also urging a united front with the bourgeois leaders of the suffrage movement, on the grounds that the struggle for enfranchisement was "a distinct and common cause for all women."

After a colorful and innovative campaign, the California referendum was won by a scant 3,500 votes. Alice Blackwell hailed the victory in the *Woman's Journal* as a victory for the allied forces of women and progressivism, "the joint forces of civic righteousness." The California suffragists were primed to follow up on victory; on the opening day of the 1913 legislature, each assemblyman and senator found a card on his desk listing seventeen bills the Women's Legislative Council wanted them to enact. The legislature passed eleven of them. California became one of the first states to pass a mothers' pension law and a minimum wage bill for women. Working women also got an eight-hour law; teachers got teachers' pensions; married women were now assured joint guardianship of their children with their husbands; social reformers got a red-light district abatement and injunction act, the raising of the legal age of consent, and a state training school for delinquent girls.

The success in California was a great boost for morale and helped to tilt more women into a commitment to suffrage. It also had the effect, however, of stimulating the movement's more obdurate opponents to organize more effectively to meet the threat. The liquor industry, which feared that a female vote would be a dry vote, had mobilized heavily in California in 1911, and though defeated there it continued to pour in funds to defeat suffrage measures. Cotton manufacturers, who employed large numbers of women and children in Southern factories, feared the reforming zeal of women, as did business in general, which was already facing the menace of progressive regulatory legislation. Moreover, formal organizations of *women* opposed to women's suffrage were also organizing, and in 1911 the National Association Opposed to Woman Suffrage was formed, with twenty-five state organizations.

These organizations never amounted to much in the way of numbers, but that they existed at all was important in terms of public opinion. The prominent members were mostly upper-class women who, like many upper-class men in this period, had doubts about mass democracy and were appalled at the prospect of extending the vote to masses of "ignorant" working-class women, immigrant and native. The arguments against women's suffrage by now usually avoided the idea that women should remain in sheltered domestic retirement: with so many women prominently engaged in public reform and club work, this was beginning to seem rather absurd. A more up-to-date and modern argument, which took into account the growth of women's activities outside the home, was that women had already been able to effect desirable reforms *without* the vote. Enfranchisement would do nothing to increase their power; in fact, by inevitably getting them involved in party politics, it might well destroy the influence they had gained by being above the party battle. Fundamentally the crux of the opposition seems to have been the need to maintain clear distinctions between men and women. As the dividing lines between male and female spheres blurred, the vote remained a potent symbolic boundary.

Alice Blackwell's idea that progressivism and the women's movement were two sides of the same coin received a boost in 1912 when Theodore Roosevelt formed a new Progressive party. Its platform had a solid number of "social justice" planks, including woman suffrage. Roosevelt wanted the endorsement of Jane Addams, by now probably the most famous woman in America, and she persuaded him that suffrage was not only desirable but important enough for the party to champion. At the convention that publicly launched the party, Roosevelt asked Addams to second his nomination. She did so before a wildly enthusiastic throng—an extraordinary occasion considering that the vast majority of women in America still could not vote.

1912 was something of a banner year for suffrage—Oregon, Kansas, and Arizona all enfranchised their women. The following year, after a strong suffrage campaign that bypassed the need for a state constitutional amendment, the Illinois legislature granted women the right to vote in presidential and local, but not state, elections. This made Illinois the first state east of the Mississippi to pass women suffrage legislation. These victories, together with Montana and Nevada in 1912–1914, helped persuade more cautious women that woman suffrage was a serious issue, and membership in the national organization swelled. In 1914 the General Federation of Women's Clubs as an organized body at last threw its weight behind suffrage; two years later so did the United Daughters of the Confederacy and the Daughters of the

American Revolution. These were major accessions of organized and influential women. By 1917 the NAWSA boasted two million members and was the largest voluntary organization in the country.

The state victories also turned NAWSA activists to a rethinking of their strategies. On the one hand, they seemed to vindicate the plan of fighting for suffrage state by state. On the other hand, the momentum that seemed to be building, and the fact that there was now a fairly large bloc of Western women who could vote, revived the hope of turning once more to the possibility of a constitutional amendment.

In 1910 the NAWSA had formed a congressional committee to keep the idea of a constitutional amendment alive, as a sideline to the main NAWSA concentration on the states, and in 1912 it was taken over by a relative newcomer to suffrage leadership, Alice Paul. Paul was a young Quaker social worker who had studied at the London School of Economics and become involved with the British suffragettes. She had even been arrested and spent some time in a British jail, where, like many of the British protesters, she had gone on a hunger strike and suffered the horrible process of force-feeding. On her return to the United States in 1910, together with another young American woman, Lucy Burns, whom she had met in jail in London, she determined to bring what she had learned in Britain to the American suffrage movement.

Paul aimed to push what she always referred to as the "Susan B. Anthony" amendment to the center of NAWSA efforts. She and Burns recruited a number of other younger women activists, who like them were impatient with what they saw as the timidity and caution of the NAWSA, and created a new body, the Congressional Union, as an "affiliate" of the parent body. Harriot Stanton Blatch joined them, and so did Crystal Eastman, Rheta Dorr, Inez Milholland, and most of the members of Heterodoxy. Paul also decided to break with the NAWSA's longstanding nonpartisan policy and adopt the British policy of holding the party in power responsible for not taking action on women's suffrage. She encouraged her followers to heckle candidates unmercifully, and urged the newly enfranchised women in the West to defeat the Democrats in the 1912 presidential election.

In 1913 Paul orchestrated a massive march in Washington, D.C., on the day the new president, Woodrow Wilson, was to arrive for his inauguration. An estimated 300,000 people gathered to watch the 5,000-strong suffrage march up Pennsylvania Avenue. Amidst considerable disorder, many of the marchers were roughed up by hostile members of the crowd. Police who were present did not intervene, a fact that led to a congressional inquiry and considerable public sympathy for the marchers. But one hostile editorial set out bluntly the usually unspoken terms of the bargain between men and women: "If women want the kind of consideration to which they have been accustomed, they must live by the conventional standards."

Paul was a woman of rigid determination and notable charisma who inspired total devotion in some and detestation in others, including NAWSA president Anna Howard Shaw. The Congressional Union's emphasis on its youth added to the friction with the NAWSA, and its brash methods dismayed the older organization's leadership. They not only found such behavior as heckling unladylike but also thought that attacking the Democrats was a bad tactic. As far as possible, the suffrage movement had hewed to a nonpartisan line; part of the image it wished to project for the woman voter was that she would not be a slave to party. In 1913 the NAWSA pushed out the CU, and Paul and her followers, together with many newly enfranchised women from the Western states, created the National Woman's party.

Since Wilson remained equivocal on the question of votes for women and stood by a states' rights position, the new party embarked on a determined policy to defeat the president and the Democrats in 1916. It did not succeed, but Paul determined that the National Woman's party should remain a thorn in the president's side. Adopting a strategy from the labor movement, the party began to picket the White House. In January 1917 squads of women rotated in a constant picket outside the gates, where they could be seen by passersby and by the president every time he left the building. They were silent, but they carried placards with slogans such as "Democracy Begins at Home." Once the United States had joined in the world war, several placards referred to the president as "Kaiser Wilson" and ceremoniously burned copies of his speeches.

Meanwhile the NAWSA was undergoing major changes. In 1915 Carrie Chapman Catt was called back to head the organization, taking over from Shaw. Paul and her followers had succeeded in drumming up new excitement about a constitutional amendment and even having it brought to debate in Congress in 1914–1915—the first time since 1887 in the Senate, and the first time ever in the House. Even though it was defeated, this was a considerable coup. Irritated as she was by Paul's methods, Catt nevertheless saw the wisdom of going all out for a constitutional amendment, and in 1916 she unveiled her "winning plan" to the NAWSA executive. First she insisted on discipline; there should be a national level of coordination among all local societies, and all plans should be cleared with the national executive in order not to waste energy and resources. The main thrust of suffrage work would be for a constitutional amendment, but the states were not to be neglected; any new state victory would not only boost morale but add to the numbers of congressmen and senators who could be expected to vote for an amendment. It would also build up the number of states who would vote "yes" when it came to ratification. Other issues of concern to many suffragists, such as protective legislation and other social reforms affecting women, would be pushed aside to allow a total concentration on the single goal of the vote. Tactical considerations now superseded all others.

Where state organizations were strong, state campaigns were

still pursued. But 1915 saw defeat in New Jersey and a particularly bitter defeat in New York after a spectacular campaign. New York suffragists tried again in 1917 with a quieter but dogged campaign in which workers collected a million female signatures to a suffrage petition, and this time they succeeded. To everyone's surprise, it was New York City that carried the state. Suffragists had not held out much hope for the city because of its large foreign-born population and large working class. An important factor in the victory, in addition to the radical political ideas of the Jewish population and some of the Italians, was the about-face of Tammany Hall, the Democratic political machine that dominated New York politics. From being resolutely against, Tammany bosses had now concluded that woman suffrage was inevitable, so they should conciliate the future woman voter. Thus they put their influence to work in the referendum. By the end of 1917, including New York, seven new states had been added to the suffrage roster.

After the 1917 victory in New York, the NAWSA could see victory ahead for the constitutional amendment, but all suffrage plans were disrupted by the U.S. entry into World War I. The outbreak of war in Europe in 1914 had come as a tremendous shock and supplied another argument for the suffrage movement—that women as mothers found war particularly abhorrent, and therefore women voters would not let the United States be sucked into the conflict. "I Didn't Raise My Boy to Be a Soldier" was a popular ballad of the period. When in February 1917 the president decided that the United States could no longer remain uninvolved in the conflict, leaders of the suffrage movement faced an acute dilemma. How should the organized suffrage movement respond? Most of the major leaders, including Catt and Paul, were committed pacifists, as was Jeannette Rankin of Montana, the only woman sitting in the House of Representatives when Congress was called upon to vote for war in April. She was one of the fifty who voted against.

In the atmosphere of militant patriotism that quickly arose

after Wilson's war announcement, was it politically feasible for the NAWSA to oppose the president? Was it even possible to keep the organization together? Some ardent feminists became staunch supporters of the war effort, among them Harriot Stanton Blatch and Charlotte Perkins Gilman, who had once thought that war was an outdated dysfunctional aspect of androcentric culture but now felt that civilization depended on defeating the "Hun." Jane Addams, on the other hand, remained committed to pacifism, and Crystal Eastman helped found a new, more "aggressive" peace party, dedicated among other things to fighting the intolerance of dissent that the war almost immediately produced.

Any hint that the NAWSA was in any way "disloyal," Catt was convinced, would kill the movement. In addition to war unity, the Bolshevik Revolution of 1917 in Russia made even the most mildly radical movements suspect. "Do you know that there is a close alliance between woman suffrage, Socialism and Feminism?" was now the propaganda ploy of groups opposed to suffrage. Catt was quick to assert that the NAWSA was "a bourgeois movement with nothing radical about it," and the organization began to dissociate itself from its prewar socialist allies.

At the same time Catt was not ready to put suffrage "on hold" for the duration. Stanton and Anthony had done that during the Civil War, convinced that a grateful Republican party would reward them after the war. They had been cruelly disappointed, and Catt was not about to make the same mistake. Her solution was to offer the services of the national organization to the administration during the emergency and to leave all the NAWSA branches free to operate in any way they thought fit in support of the war effort—but at the same time to maintain a steady pressure on Congress and the president in support of the Anthony amendment. Women were acting as citizens in their support for the war effort; they should be treated as citizens by being given the vote. When Wilson publicly declared that the conflict was a war for democracy, he played into the suffragists' hands. Catt urged the president to create a more perfect democracy in the United States by at last granting universal suffrage as a war measure.

Alice Paul, on the other hand, refused to compromise an inch. Much to the disgust of Catt and Blatch, she refused to withdraw the pickets from the White House. While they had been a mere curiosity before America entered the war, their silent presence and their placards now seemed to many bystanders as near treason; hostile crowd reactions, even violence, led to the arrest not of the mob but of the pickets—for obstructing the sidewalk. By November 1917, 218 women had been arrested and 97 sentenced to jail, where some went on hunger strikes and were subjected to force-feeding. If the pickets embarrassed the president, their arrest and the appalling jail conditions they endured embarrassed him even more, and drew enough public sympathy that all were released by the end of the year.

Meanwhile the war was opening new opportunities for women. Even before America's entry, the steady flow of armaments orders from Britain and France had produced an expansion in the economy while the sudden halt of immigration brought a tightening of the labor supply. White women and black male workers, and to a lesser extent African-American women, found new and better-paying jobs now open to them. Women worked in munitions factories, in chemical plants, and in such highly visible jobs as streetcar conductors. A number of war industry factories even set up nurseries where women workers could leave their children. A 1920 report from the Connecticut Department of Labor claimed that both the children's health and their habits improved due to their experience of "scientific" care, but this did not lead to any widespread postwar drive for on-site nurseries for working mothers. The expansion of female labor opportunities seldom brought into the labor market women who had never worked at all; rather it meant that working women now had the chance to move from their old "women's" jobs to "men's" jobs—with male paychecks.

The war also enhanced opportunities for women reformers to continue their prewar interests. Mary van Kleeck and Josephine Goldmark, for example, were employed on a federal government committee to coordinate and oversee the integration of women workers into the war economy. From this position they sought to extend the job opportunities opening to women while protecting them from exploitation, though Goldmark admitted that it was difficult "to stand for the rights of women and also for their protection." In 1920, responding to pressure from the WTUL and other women's groups, Congress converted the committee into a permanent Women's Bureau in the Department of Labor, with Mary Anderson, who had been an organizer for the WTUL, at its head.

While most women participated in the war effort in traditional ways, through membership in the Red Cross or conserving food, a few made a more direct military contribution. The army was anxious to recruit trained nurses and dispatched several thousand to France, but it would not employ African-American nurses, and it steadfastly refused to send women doctors. A number of women physicians did eventually get to Europe, but only because they went independently and at their own expense. Other women went overseas as Salvation Army workers or for the YWCA. A number of wealthy women expatriates outfitted their own ambulance units or supported hospitals; women drivers were recruited to deliver supplies and generally offer transport either at home or in France; a number of young wealthy women sent over their own cars.

Thus for some American women the war briefly offered unprecedented opportunities. And a number of social programs that had been dear to many women could be pursued as part of the war effort. The Children's Bureau in 1918 began a program to register new births throughout the country and to weigh and measure young children as a way to detect medical problems early. Women who had been concerned about prostitution now had the strong cooperation of the army, which was determined to protect its fighting men from the perils of sex and particularly from venereal disease, and kept a tight cordon around army camps, summarily arresting girls and women who might appear to be prostitutes.

Both the picketing and the quieter work of the NAWSA prevented suffrage from being completely swamped by the war. The growing number of states with women suffrage in 1917 meant that politicians now had to take women's voting power into account. By 1918 seventeen states had already granted women suffrage. The NAWSA's two million members should have been enough to demonstrate to practical politicians that the suffrage cause had a critical mass of supporters. Most women might remain indifferent, but Catt and the NAWSA leadership were no longer interested in the wholesale transformation of women nor even by now in the conversion of large numbers of men. The final phase of their campaign would be relentless pressure carried out by dedicated, thoroughly prepared groups of suffrage women in Washington, lobbying the professional politicians in Congress and the White House, where power lay.

Their model was the success of the Anti-Saloon League, the male organization that by the 1910s had surpassed the WCTU as the most effective agent for prohibition. Unlike the women's organization, the Anti-Saloon League had never been interested in grass-roots revivalist transformation; it had operated as a high-powered, efficiently organized lobbying group concentrated on Washington—and by 1918 it had achieved the Eighteenth Amendment to the Constitution.

The crucial factor for suffrage was that by 1918 President Wilson had been won over and was ready to throw his weight behind an amendment. On January 10, 1918, the amendment came to a vote in the House and passed by exactly the necessary two-thirds majority. The final vote there has become part of suffrage folklore, with congressmen rousing themselves from sickbeds to fulfill their commitment to vote Yea, and the women watching intently from the gallery breaking into a hymn as the final tally was announced. The Senate was harder to persuade; in spite of Wilson's pressure, even his appeal in person in the Senate chamber, the Senate rejected the amendment by two votes.

The issue did not come up again until June 1919; by this time the war was over, and Britain and Canada had already enfranchised their women. President Wilson, in Paris for the peace talks, nonetheless maintained pressure, and this time, on June 4, the Senate voted 56 to 25 for the amendment. The battle was not yet won, since to become law the amendment had to be ratified by two-thirds, or thirty-six, of the states. During 1919 six more states came over to suffrage, either by constitutional amendment or by legislative enactment, so that by the time the Anthony amendment went to the states, thirty states already had women suffrage and ratified as a matter of course. Others followed, but by June 1920 the suffrage forces were still one state short.

Catt was determined that women across the nation should be able to vote in the 1920 election, but time was running out. It was Wilson who pressured the governor of Tennessee into calling a special session of the state legislature to vote upon ratification. Nashville became an almost carnival scene as suffragists and their most determined opponents descended en masse on the small city to lobby the state legislature, and the nation's press arrived in droves to report on the crucial battle. When the youngest member of the state legislature, Harry Burn, changed his "no" vote to "yes" on August 18, apparently on the appeal of his mother, Tennessee became the thirty-sixth state to ratify.

With the narrow decision in Tennessee, the Nineteenth Amendment to the Constitution was ratified; being female was no longer a barrier to voting anywhere in the United States. A number of other states that still had not ratified now did so, but nine Southern states held out as a matter of principle, though this made no difference to their women's ability to exercise the franchise. Virginia did not ratify until 1952, Mississippi until 1984. This "principled" reluctance points up what active suffragists had always known, even if they did not always express it publicly in the heat of the battle. The young Florence Luscomb, trying to explain in 1914 why men for so long had dug in their heels against giving women the vote, echoed the sentiment of the African-American poet Angelina Weld Grimké: woman suffrage stood "for a more significant change. . . . It symbolizes equality."

Many historians have tended to downplay the importance of winning the vote. It did not bring complete equality between men and women. It did not usher in an era of social justice—indeed, women had achieved more along those lines in the early twentieth century without the vote than they would for some time with it. It could not be said to have measurably improved the lives of the poorest and most vulnerable women, and most African-American women in the South were not even able to exercise it. Yet without it, women, whatever power or privileges some enjoyed, were set apart as civil inferiors. "To be left out by the State," a working woman explained, "just sets up a prejudice against us. Bosses think and women come to think themselves that they don't count as much as men."

The importance of the ballot is confirmed by the doggedness of the resistance to granting it and the length of time it took to obtain it. In only thirteen states did a majority of male voters ever approve woman suffrage in a referendum. The rest came either by legislative enactment (nine states in 1919)—that is, through the decisions of the political elite of professional politicians—or through acquiescence in the constitutional amendment. As Carrie Chapman Catt pointed out in 1926, the acknowledgment of equal citizenship signified by the vote "cost the women of the country fifty-two years of pauseless campaign. . . . Young suffragists who helped forge the last links of that chain were not born when it began. The suffragists who forged the first links were dead when it ended."

# 6

## After the Vote

May you both live until children will wonder what could have been the necessity of a meeting like this.—Clara Barton to Elizabeth Cady Stanton and Susan B. Anthony, on a women's rights convention, 1869

AS CLARA BARTON'S remark implies, from one perspective the ultimate triumph of the women's rights movement would be signaled by its withering away from sheer lack of discrimination to combat, leaving behind not a venerated heroic myth but a blank incomprehension as to what all the fuss could have been about. Neither Stanton nor Anthony lived to see such a consummation, but by the late 1920s their successors did find themselves in a world in which the blank incomprehension was rather prematurely evident.

For the women who had given much of their lives to the Cause, the victory of the Nineteenth Amendment brought both elation and the realization that probably nothing that would ever happen to them would equal the meaning and shape that had been given to their lives by the long campaign. "It leaves its mark on one, such a struggle," recalled Carrie Chapman Catt in her memoir of the suffrage movement. "It fills the days and it rides the nights." At the last convention of the NAWSA in February

1920, which had been both a wild victory celebration and the funeral of the old organization, the celebrants could not shake off
the feeling that something had gone from their lives forever. "It
made them stop one another in corridors and in corners to whis-
per, 'To think that we shall not meet again like this—not next
year, not ever!'"

In the election of 1920 only one person was still alive who had
signed the 1848 Declaration of Sentiments in which women
made their first formal demand for the ballot. Charlotte Wood-
ward had been nineteen when she had attended the Seneca Falls
meeting and put her name to the declaration; now, at ninety-one,
she cast her first vote. The only remaining member of the old
pre–Civil War leadership was Antoinette Brown Blackwell, who
had joined the movement in the early 1850s when she was in her
twenties. At the age of ninety-five she rode in state in an open
carriage to cast her vote.

The actual turnout of enfranchised women in the 1920 vote
was somewhat disappointing: anywhere from 35 percent of those
eligible to just under 50 percent. Although commentators often
blamed the decline of voter turnout in the 1920s on the failure of
women to take advantage of their new privilege, voting had been
declining among men too for some years. The decline of real
party competition in many parts of the country made politics less
exciting and compelling to many men, and there seemed to be no
issues in 1920 that were sufficiently galvanizing to overcome the
shyness or traditional mores or sheer inertia of many women.
Reluctance was strongest among working-class and immigrant
women, where actions that transgressed traditional gender
boundaries were likely to receive decisive disapproval from husbands or other female family members. But elite women who
had actively campaigned against the vote, now that they had
it, were quite ready to use it. In the Southern states, African-
American women were soon disfranchised by the same methods
as their menfolk, but in the rest of the country black women
showed considerable interest in politics and may even have regis-

tered to vote in higher proportions than white women. Overall, however, female voting continued to lag, and it was not until 1956 that the percentage of women voting equaled men's.

With the passage of the Nineteenth Amendment, Catt reformed the NAWSA into the League of Women Voters, convinced that women needed education in citizenship and could be a vital force for the education of others. But Catt was an experienced politician, and she had no illusions as to the role of power in politics and where it lay. In her inaugural address as president of the League, she warned her audience that "the only way to get things in this country is from the inside of the political parties." Unless women could penetrate them, they would remain "auxiliaries." She warned that "there are inner circles in the parties where you will not be wanted, but it is just there that you must go. . . . You have a struggle ahead."

And so it turned out. Crystal Eastman believed that "after all these centuries of retirement women need more than an 'equal opportunity' to show what's in them. They need a generous shove into positions of responsibility." They were not about to get it from the major parties. Republicans and Democrats appointed women to national committees, but it soon became clear that much of this was window dressing. Emily Newell Blair, who was appointed vice chair of the Democratic National Committee in 1921, became increasingly disillusioned with the parties' commitment to women. She believed the party managers handpicked women who would be docile and accommodating. Male politicos were happy to use women in the detailed work of party politics as canvassers, speakers, poll watchers, or party headquarters staff, but women who were interested in office and political power soon found themselves kept on the periphery. Parties nominated women only for seats they knew were lost; the inner circles, where real decisions were made, remained for men only.

Until 1933, no more than thirteen women served in the House of Representatives, and seven of them were there by a kind of

family succession as widows of former incumbents. In state legislatures the number of women peaked at the end of the twenties
and tapered off with the depression. Congress did, however, create the Women's Bureau, staffed by women, in the Department
of Labor in 1920 as a watchdog for women's working conditions.
It joined the Children's Bureau as bastions of women's influence
and some power in the still overwhelmingly masculine world of
Washington. President Warren Harding also appointed the suffragist Helen Gardener as the only woman on the Civil Service
Commission, and women managed for the first time to gain full
admission to all civil service examinations, though the Veterans'
Preference Act after the war still put women at a considerable
disadvantage.

Few of the leaders of the suffrage movement had personal
ambition for political power. Carrie Chapman Catt, who was a
consummate politician, devoted the rest of her life to the peace
movement. Many of the younger activists, however, had political
agendas they were determined to pursue. The suffrage movement had activated a great many women who presumably would
be a ready constituency for further advances. At the same time
the pursuit of suffrage, while necessary, had pushed aside other
goals that were nearer to their hearts. Katherine Anthony in
1921 put it bluntly: "Now that suffrage is out of the way, there is
a great need for the broader kind of feminism." Crystal Eastman
declared simply in August 1920, as the Nineteenth Amendment
was being ratified: "Now we can begin!"

Eastman had an agenda in mind for a postsuffrage feminist
movement that would incorporate the individual psychic liberation she felt was at the heart of a true feminism along with a solid
program of needed social reform. Now that suffrage was won,
women could pursue what they were really after, and "what they
are really after . . . is *freedom*." But freedom was not only multi-
faceted, it was rather complicated. Women needed a "free soul,"
she wrote, a "certain emotional freedom, a strong healthy ego-
tism, and some un-personal sources of joy." But this was not

something the individual could generate entirely from within herself. "Conditions of outward freedom" must be created "in which a free woman's soul can be born and grow. It is these outward conditions with which an organized feminist movement must concern itself." Among these "conditions of outward freedom," she listed the real opening of all the professions to women, a more androgynous early socialization of boys and girls, government endowment of motherhood, and easily available birth control.

Many reform-minded feminists were less concerned with individual liberation than with a continuing agenda of social reform to benefit poorer women and children. In 1920 a number of women's organizations joined forces to form the Women's Joint Congressional Committee, chaired by the experienced suffrage lobbyist Maud Wood Park, to push for legislation of concern to women. The committee's first priority was the Sheppard-Towner Bill, then stalled in Congress. It would provide health care for the underserved poor and rural mothers and young children of America, as a way of dealing with the exceptionally high rate of child and maternal death. The measure grew out of an investigation by the Children's Bureau into maternal and infant death, and had first been introduced in 1918 by Jeannette Rankin. The bill was seen as very much a woman's issue, and something which the new electorate might have close to heart. When Senator James Reed of Missouri made a crack about the "old maids" who would be staffing the new organization, Senator William Kenyon of Iowa shot back: "The old maids are voting now."

The Sheppard-Towner Act, passed in 1920, was a major departure because it established a direct federal responsibility for welfare. Appropriations of federal funds went to the states to set up agencies for maternal education, well-baby clinics, and visiting nurses to see mothers in their homes. A major supporter was Dr. Josephine Baker, who declared that the infant welfare station should be as natural a part of public functions as the public school or public library. The act was immediately denounced as Communist-inspired, and a cautious Congress provided that funding would expire in 1927 unless it was explicitly renewed. Under attack from the American Medical Association, the continued charge of socialism, and accusations that public money was being wasted to allow old maids to interfere between mothers and their children, the act was in fact allowed to expire in 1929. But for a brief time it established an innovative scheme of preventive health care, largely staffed by public health nurses and women physicians.

As the ultimate fate of the Sheppard-Towner Act revealed, the social and political climate changed dramatically during the twenties. By mid-decade women reformers were finding that they could no longer count on the progressive tide to lift them and their causes along. Being a socialist now brought one under grave suspicion, and even after the demise of the postwar Red Scare there was substantial paranoia about communism and the left in general. A "spider's web" chart originating in the Department of Chemical Warfare purported to show how most of the major women's organizations, peace groups, and principal social reformers, including Florence Kelley and Jane Addams, formed an interlocking directorate linked to international communism. By the mid-twenties crucial reform allies such as the General Federation of Women's Clubs were turning away from activism; the DAR, which had been an early supporter of Sheppard-Towner, had withdrawn its support by 1922 and became increasingly right-wing, drawing up a list of suspect groups that included the WCTU and the YWCA along with individuals like Jane Addams and the women of the Children and Women's bureaus. The National Association Opposed to Woman Suffrage reconstituted itself as a superpatriotic, anti-socialist, anti-feminist group with an effective journal, the *Woman Patriot*. The acquired habits of public activism carried some women in the Midwest quite easily from work in the suffrage movement to involvement in the revived Ku Klux Klan.

In the early twenties women continued to press specific equality rights. Activists lobbied state governments to make sure that enfranchisement would include women's eligibility for jury duty. Many states were in fact quite reluctant to make that automatic connection, and courts resisted extending by implication the effect of the Nineteenth Amendment to eligibility for jury duty. By the early 1940s still only twenty-eight states allowed women to sit on juries, and most of these allowed very generous exemptions to women.

One small but symbolically significant victory of the period was the passage of the Cable Act in 1922, regularizing the citizenship of American women who married foreign men. Since 1855 the American man had possessed the quasi-feudal power of being able automatically to bestow citizenship upon a foreign wife, as on his children. On the assumption that a woman naturally assumed the nationality of her husband, however, an American woman marrying a foreigner automatically forfeited her American citizenship. Now that women were enfranchised, this meant that a woman with an unnaturalized foreign husband would not be able to vote. Harriot Stanton Blatch was one suffragist who could not have voted in the 1920 election if the sudden accidental death of her British husband in 1915 had not restored her American citizenship. The Cable Act equalized the situation of men and women; neither could bestow citizenship upon a foreign spouse, and neither lost his or her citizenship upon marrying a foreigner, though a woman's status changed to that of a naturalized, rather than a native-born, citizen.

The act did not affect a great many women, but it was important to feminists because it removed one of the last remnants of *couverture* in which a woman's private, semi-feudal allegiance to a husband took precedence over a public allegiance to the state. Like all "equality" measures, this one too had its downside for some; whereas in the old dispensation immigrant women automatically became citizens when their husbands did, now they had to make the effort to apply and qualify for citizenship independently.

Since jury duty was likely to be regarded by most women as a chore rather than a right, and because the Cable Act affected comparatively few people, neither of these causes could be the basis for a new postsuffrage mass movement. The League of Women Voters became an enduring and worthy institution, but it never became the engine of a mass women's movement—nor did it intend to be, and membership declined precipitously from the old NAWSA. Florence Luscomb said unkindly of the Boston branch of the League: "Individually they are all lovely women: collectively, they have the energy of a mud turtle." She was one young feminist who wanted desperately to find a movement as compelling as suffrage, "to get into the next fight of the future," but she was not at all sure what that might be, though instinctively she felt it would have to do with the labor question and "industrial democracy." Anna Howard Shaw had pointed out before her death that with the victory of suffrage, "you have lost your symbol. There is nothing for the women to rally around." What could take its place?

One possibility for a renewed and revitalized feminist coalition might have been to follow the lead of African-American women activists and reestablish the link between race and sex equality. When voter registration opened for the 1920 election in the major cities of the South, a number of determined black women turned up and succeeded in registering despite official delays and prevarications. Ironically this redounded to the benefit of white women, since Democratic politicians who had always opposed woman suffrage now suddenly began an all-out effort to get reluctant white women to register.

In most areas of the South, election officials quickly recovered from their initial shock and began to implement the same barriers that kept most African-American men from voting, primarily rigged "literacy" tests. A number of prominent African-

American women appealed to both the League of Women Voters and the National Women's party for aid in protesting the obstructions to their exercise of the vote, and for support of their agitation for an anti-lynching bill, the major legislative initiative of the National Association of Colored Women's Clubs.

But this was not an issue that appealed to many white activists, especially not to Alice Paul. She insisted that the NACW was a race, not a feminist, organization, and that questions of the effective disfranchisement of black women in the South, or of lynching, were race issues that should be quite distinct from the woman concerns of the NWP. Paul had always been elusive on the question of racial equality; Mary Church Terrell later wrote bitterly that she was convinced that if Alice Paul could have got the suffrage amendment through Congress without enfranchising black women, she would have. Nor were these issues welcome at the League of Women Voters; African-American women who appealed to the new organization to take up the cause of disfranchisement were rebuffed, and black women were not welcome as members.

Another cause of widespread significance that might have been the foundation for a broad-based movement was birth control. Crystal Eastman considered birth control a necessary part of a broad feminist agenda, but in fact almost every section of the feminist movement shied away from it. Both Margaret Sanger and Mary Ware Dennett urged the NWP to make it part of its program, but without success. Alice Paul felt that this issue was too divisive and would distract from the single-minded pursuit of her own pet project of an equal-rights amendment. In vain, Sanger argued that the NWP had an extremely narrow conception of what "equal rights" meant. How could women have equal rights with men as long as they were denied "the right to control their own bodies"? The League of Women Voters was equally reluctant, deciding that birth control did not belong "among women citizens' concerns." Just as the fear of Southern reaction deterred white women's organizations from taking up questions of race, now fear of Roman Catholic women's opposition made them steer clear of birth control.

The Children's Bureau also considered birth control too controversial to handle. The bureau refused to give any information on contraception to women who wrote asking for advice, or even to refer them to the American Birth Control League. The health services offered to poor women under the Sheppard-Towner Act did not include information on birth control. In the postwar atmosphere of growing conservatism, in which the accusation of bolshevism or socialism was a real threat, the women of the Children's Bureau did not wish to endanger their budgets or their marginal position in the federal government.

Mary Ware Dennett continued to try, without success, to get the Comstock laws amended to remove contraception from the definition of obscenity, as a free-speech issue and on the grounds that contraception was an entirely private matter over which the government should have no control. She also opposed allowing access to be controlled by the medical profession. Sanger, on the other hand, was convinced that this was a losing proposition. "You . . . are interested in an abstract idea," she wrote to Dennett, "I am interested in women, in their lives."

Sanger had found a loophole in the judge's argument at her 1917 trial for opening a birth-control clinic. The judge had allowed that it was permissible for doctors to prescribe contraception for the "cure and prevention of disease." Backed by the support of wealthy women like Elsie Parsons and Katharine Houghton Hepburn, as well as by her new husband, the industrialist J. Noah Slee, Sanger seized the opportunity to open a Clinical Research Bureau in New York. It was staffed by physicians and dispensed contraceptives mainly to poor married women for whom some reasonable medical reason could be found against childbearing. The clinic also amassed a good deal of valuable research on contraception.

Gradually Sanger was winning over key medical men, though the American Medical Association did not officially endorse contraception until 1937. Sanger herself had come round to the idea that contraception was an essentially medical process and should be controlled by licensed physicians alone, partly because she feared the havoc that might be created by quack remedies if information were made entirely free. Moreover the determined hostility of the medical profession had been one of the major elements in terminating the Sheppard-Towner experiment; Sanger realized that only by making the medical profession guardians of contraception for women would it be possible to legalize birth control at all. By the late thirties, this was the direction that the final legalization of birth control took. It meant that contraception would be placed in the context of the preservation of women's health, and later of population control, rather than of women's freedom to choose. It would be divorced from any broad feminist ideology.

In February 1921 the National Women's party met in convention to decide its future. The delegates began with the ceremonial presentation to Congress of a marble collective bust of the original heroines of the movement—Susan B. Anthony, Elizabeth Cady Stanton, and Lucretia Mott. Congress did not quite know what to do with this gift, and it ended up gathering dust in the capitol basement. Alice Paul and her inner circle had already decided that the new equivalent to suffrage would be another amendment to the Constitution guaranteeing no discrimination on the basis of sex. Such an amendment, like the vote, would provide one clear goal which would weld at least a dedicated corps of the old movement together for common action.

Crystal Eastman had already presented Paul with her own more comprehensive plan, covering the legalization of birth control, expanded mothers' pensions, and the reform of marriage laws so that the status of the homemaker wife should cease to be that of a dependent "entitled to her board and keep in return for her services" and be acknowledged as a full partner. Paul responded impatiently: "Yes, I believe in all these things, but I am not interested in writing a fine program. I am interested in getting something done."

Getting something done, she was convinced, required unity and clarity of focus. After much consultation with lawyers, Paul thrashed out a formulary for an equal-rights amendment (ERA). The aim was to remove all legal disabilities affecting women through the simple stroke of a constitutional amendment, which would establish the principle of gender equality. Its implications could then be worked out and elaborated in the courts. A very basic problem immediately brought up by people like Florence Kelley and women trade unionists was whether such an amendment would not invalidate special protective labor laws for women. Several lawyers had in fact warned Paul that a blanket amendment of this kind would provide a conservative court with a ready opening to invalidate sex-specific legislation. Although Paul had earlier favored protective legislation, she was increasingly influenced by Gail Laughlin of the newly formed National Federation of Business and Professional Women's Clubs, who argued that protection was just another barrier for women in the economic struggle, a way for male unionists to keep women out of well-paying jobs.

Paul formally unveiled the proposed equal-rights amendment in November 1923 at Seneca Falls, to commemorate the seventy-fifth anniversary of the Declaration of Sentiments. It was introduced into Congress in December. The original wording was; "Men and women shall have equal rights throughout the United States and every place subject to its jurisdiction," but in 1943 this was modified to the current formulation, echoing the phraseology of the Fifteenth and Nineteenth Amendments: "Equality of rights under the law shall not be denied or abridged by the United States or by any state on account of sex."

An immediate barrage of opposition was aimed at Congress from labor organizations and from the Women's Bureau. After a massive investigation of the effect of labor legislation on women's employment and opportunities, the bureau concluded that hours and other protective legislation did not hamper women's ability to gain employment, and that minimum wages did not degenerate into maximums. The dispute became extremely bitter. Florence Kelley, who had been a member of the National Women's party, resigned over the issue; long-standing friendships were broken. Maud Wood Park had warned Paul, "You will divide the woman's movement." And she did.

Protectionists accused the NWP of being a tool of business and catering only to rich and professional women who had no need of protection. NWP spokeswomen replied that unions were protesting the ERA and supporting protection because it kept women from competing with men for better-paid jobs, and that much of their concern about women's health was sheer hypocrisy. "What working-class mother of small children ever had nine hours' consecutive rest?" demanded Crystal Eastman derisively. "What traditional union husband ever felt that it was his concern to see that she should have?"

While Kelley and the Women's Bureau emphasized the destructive effects on poor and vulnerable women if the protections of hours and wages laws were withdrawn, Paul and the NWP cited the women, such as printers and streetcar conductors, who lost their jobs because the law did not allow them to work at night or do overtime. Or the women who could not be employed at skilled, well-paying jobs because employers would not accommodate the restrictions on their hours. It did not help heal the breach that the National Association of Manufacturers rushed to endorse the ERA, and that in the same year the Supreme Court in *Adkins v. Children's Hospital* (1923) invalidated a minimum-wage law for women, using among its arguments that since enfranchisement, women were now "equal" with men and did not need the paternalistic protection of the state in making contracts for employment.

The NWP's hard-line stand on the ERA decisively alienated many ex-suffragists and reform-minded women. NWP membership, which had been between 35,000 and 60,000 in 1919–1920, rapidly dwindled to around 10,000. Those 10,000, however, contained some very high-profile women, such as Alva Belmont, who became the party's president and its financial angel in 1924; the aviator Amelia Earhart; the poet Edna St. Vincent Millay; the movie star Gloria Swanson; Bryn Mawr college president M. Cary Thomas; and Mrs. William Randolph Hearst, among others. Proponents of the ERA, however high profile, were a small minority; the mass of organized women opposed it. The Children's Bureau joined the Women's Bureau as an active opponent within the federal bureaucracy. The WTUL, the National Consumers' League, and the new League of Women Voters all were opposed. Although the ERA was reintroduced into Congress in 1924, 1925, and 1929, the concerted opposition of so many at hearings prevented it from ever being reported favorably out of committee.

Unlike later quarrels over the ERA, this was not a dispute between feminists and traditional, conservative women. It was a dispute within the heart of the feminist community. It reflected a difference that had always been present between those women who came to women's rights or feminism from a yearning to break free of the "bonds of womanhood" and saw gender as less important than individuality, and those who had an intense awareness of the different qualities and problems of women. The former not only thought that protective legislation worked in the end against women's interests, but that it diminished women's own sense of self and encouraged them to think of themselves as weak. Harriot Stanton Blatch thought working women were being led astray by welfare workers, that "it was the welfare worker who was holding up to them the inferiority complex." Opponents tended to regard working women essentially as mothers and to be more acutely aware of their burdens than their possibilities.

Opponents accused Alice Paul and her colleagues of being impractical ideologues who were prepared to sacrifice real women

to a rarefied ideal of equality. They were right in the sense that
Paul and her supporters were thinking in terms both of first
principles and long-term possibilities. But Blatch had caught
something too: that many of the opponents brought an essentially social-work perspective to the dispute. They tended to be
women, like Kelley, who had spent a lifetime immersed in the
real, often overwhelming, problems of working women, and inevitably had much of their own identity invested in the structure
of protection they had helped to build. "I must as a practical person," declared Alice Hamilton, "familiar with the great inarticu-
late body of working women, reiterate my belief that they are
largely helpless, that they have very special needs which unaided
they cannot attain. . . ." To Kelley the fact of motherhood, and
the welfare of children, demanded that women be treated differently; "equality" would be positively harmful unless it was tailored to fit present realities rather than a dream future. "So long
as men cannot be mothers, so long legislation adequate for them
can never be adequate for wage-earning women; and the cry
Equality, Equality, where Nature had created Inequality, is as
stupid and as deadly as the cry Peace, Peace, where there is no
Peace."

In a letter to *The Nation* in November 1924, Crystal Eastman
strongly defended the importance of principle: "The principle of
the Equal Rights Amendment is supremely important. The very
passion with which it is opposed suggests that it is vital. To blot
out of every law book in the land, to sweep out of every dusty
court-room, to erase from every judge's mind the centuries-old
precedents to woman's inferiority and dependence and need for
protection, to substitute for it at one blow the simple new prece-
dent of equality that is a fight worth making if it takes ten years."
She thought it was psychologically important that women cease
to be classified with children and minors, and cease to think of
themselves as a vulnerable, less than fully adult class of people.
"The equal rights amendment will have a wonderful effect not

only on the attitude of men toward women, but of women toward women."

As the *New York Times* pointed out in a thoughtful 1920 article, "unlike suffrage, questions of human welfare can seldom be
answered by a categorical yes or no." They were difficult problems that required "openness to evidence, accurate foresight and
wise tolerance." But both Paul and her opponents had progressively hardened their positions and were not prepared to thrash
out a compromise.

By the late twenties there was a rush to judgment on the
achievements of the feminist movement, which assumed that it
was dead and that its leaders had often been pathetically mistaken if not downright perverse. This attitude could be seen almost immediately after the election of 1920, when commentators
were quick to blame the newly enfranchised women for the low
percentage of the enlarged electorate that actually turned out to
vote. A major study by political scientists on nonvoters indicted
women for their "inertia," and even the League of Women Voters' journal, *The Woman Citizen*, featured an article in 1924 asking, "Is Woman Suffrage Failing?" The muckraking journalist
Ida Tarbell, who had always been lukewarm about suffrage,
joined the chorus of: "Is Woman Suffrage a Failure?" but gave a
cautious endorsement. "I want to say that I believe something
has happened—something rather more in the time than I at least
thought probable—and that something is spreading." She noted
that as she moved about the country she met more women who
seemed interested and informed about current affairs and would
turn the conversation to such topics as the League of Nations or
the regulation of industry. In any case, she concluded, "political
experience must be judged not by decades, but rather by centuries. In fifty years from now we may certainly be able to ap-
praise woman's suffrage fairly—we certainly can not now."

But the assumption of feminist "failure" seems to have been
widespread among many veterans of the movement themselves,

not just their enemies. This was partly the realization that after 1920 there ceased to be a large "movement" united around a clear goal; womanhood had fragmented into thousands of differing component parts, with little sense of sisterhood remaining. But what had created "womanhood" in the first place was essentially the common experience of discrimination and confinement, symbolized by the exclusion from full citizenship. Once that blanket discrimination was removed, once women were no longer seen as properly confined to the same domestic space, it was inevitable that the unity should dissolve. Indeed, it might be seen as a mark of the success of the original impetus for the whole feminist movement that it was now possible for "Woman" to be fractured into individual women.

Older feminists found themselves misunderstood and their example rejected by younger women, who took for granted the freedoms and opportunities the elders had fought for. But, as "Feminist—New Style" wrote in *Harper's* in 1927, it was the young women in their twenties and thirties "who are the truly modern ones," and the writer was anxious to make plain to men that these young women were quite distinct from the old-style feminists. Although independent and anxious for self-expression, they did not "bear a grudge against men," and they were not about to harangue men with feminist diatribes. On the whole, the new-style feminist "enjoys working with men, more than with women." She fully expected to have a husband and children but also a career, and she had no intention of sinking herself in either; she aspired to a "well-balanced life." She felt "no loyalty to women en masse" but also knew that "her sex are in the vanguard of change." It is noteworthy that she did not repudiate the title of "feminist" but made clear that to her it meant "her American, her twentieth-century birthright to emerge from a creature of instinct into a full-fledged individual who is capable of molding her own life."

Older feminists were often discouraged by the apparent frivolity and "selfishness" of the young generation of the 1920s, their sexual freedom and their apparent lack of a social conscience. They were dismayed when young women blithely explained, "We're not out to benefit society. . . . We're out for Mary's job and Luellas's art and Barbara's independence and the rest of our individual careers and desires." Yet the fact that they could entertain such ambitions at all, and (over)confidently envisage them as possible of fulfillment, was in itself a tribute to how far women had traveled over the preceding eighty years.

In 1909 Crystal Eastman's mother, herself an ordained minister, had written to her daughter applauding her decision to become a lawyer. "If the *main contention* of the progressive woman is her right to a work of her own—a life work—then you are doing more to prove the rightness of that contention by making your way in a regular business than you could do by the most brilliant success as a social worker or investigator for a few years before marriage." Similarly, when in the mid-twenties the Bureau of Vocational Information sponsored a study of "Marriage and Careers," looking at a hundred professional women who were also wives and mothers, it justified concentrating on the professional woman because she "probably represents the advance guard in any attempt to cope with woman's present-day problems, her experience assumes high significance to all women."

Just as W. E. B. Du Bois believed that the achievements of the "Talented Tenth" of African Americans would ultimately destroy the assumption of black inferiority, even if they had no immediate ameliorative effect on the mass of black Americans, women too in the 1920s did not necessarily divorce individual achievement from wider social significance. Yet it is difficult to know how far this worked. Amelia Earhart became an American heroine by flying the Atlantic solo; yet how far did her signal achievement alter the opinion of most men about the abilities of women, including the women in their immediate circle, or of employers about employing women in responsible jobs, or even of women's attitudes about their own abilities and possibilities?

Earhart's fame certainly did not open up jobs in the burgeoning field of aviation to women except as stewardesses.

Much of the dissatisfaction of many of the old guard with the young was because the revolution of manners and morals they had mistrusted before the war seemed to have become in the 1920s an epidemic. "This is the woman's century, the first chance for the mother of the world to rise to her full place, her transcendent power to remake humanity, to rebuild the suffering world," wrote a disgusted Charlotte Perkins Gilman, "—and the world waits while she powders her nose." What disturbed Jane Addams was not so much the frivolity but what she perceived as the conformity of young people, especially college students—"a dread of change, in a desire to play safe and to let well enough alone." Rheta Dorr, on the other hand, was more hopeful about the young women of the twenties, just because they seemed to her tougher than the "helpless, clinging, ignorant little animals of my youth." They were not desperately glomming onto a man as a meal ticket, and they were determined to have a career *and* marriage and children.

For most women, this did not turn out to be any easier after 1920 than it had been in the 1910s, though, as the Bureau of Vocational Information pointed out, by 1920 there were 124,000 married professional women, an increase of 40 percent over 1910. The bureau's survey of how women juggled both jobs was directed at the "scores of eager girls" just leaving college who were wondering how to combine marriage and career. It aimed to offer "the actual experiences of women who are reaching out for and gathering all the fruits of life." This was a deliberately upbeat survey in which the author concluded that the 100 women she interviewed were happier—and so were their husbands and children—because they combined outside work with family. On the other hand, while the subjects were not rich, only 9 of the 100 had no domestic servant, and all seemed to have had highly cooperative husbands.

By the date of this study, 1926, readers were more likely to be bombarded with tales of wives who had destroyed their family life by attempting to follow an outside career and either had awakened just in time or were living filled with regrets; or of women who had followed the lure of career and given up the possibility of marriage and children and were now ruing their barren lives. This made good copy, but the reality seems to have been that women were not so much disillusioned with the idea of career-and-family as defeated by the difficulties of working it out in practice.

*The Nation* in 1927 featured a telling little vignette of the problems attached to "Trying to Be Modern." The writer was a college graduate who had been president of her college's Feminist Forum. She became a social worker in New York and right after the war was engaged to a young man with a well-established business in a small Illinois town. The realities were that she could not support him on her $125-a-month salary as a social worker in New York; he could support her on the profits of his business in small-town Illinois. She moved. The town had a population of 1,308 and absolutely no need for a professional social worker. They had children. "Part-time jobs for educated women may be developing in cities. They are few and far between in rural and small-town America." She hated housework and felt stifled, and none of her female neighbors could imagine why. Eventually she picked up a job writing a column for a small city newspaper, which she could do at home while caring for her children and coping with neighbors who would persist in dropping in. She considered it her lifeline.

Most commentators on the marriage-and-job question assumed the priority of the marriage and queried the extent to which a job could be added without harming the family. On the other hand, Martha Carey Thomas, president of Bryn Mawr, reversed the priorities and wondered to what extent marriage could be coupled with a job without detracting from *it*. In 1932 she wrote imperiously to her about-to-be-married niece, hoping that she and her husband would be able to contribute to "the all important burning question of whether a married woman can hold down a job as successfully as an unmarried woman. This must be proved over and over again before the woman question can get much further and I have set my heart on your making a success of it and so bringing great help to the 'Cause.'"

Many employers were certainly reluctant to employ married women for fear that their minds would be only half on the job. For the wife who wanted, or felt she needed, to work, the problem was not only the lack of institutional support for working married women, but the lack of psychological support. Public opinion on the whole still disapproved of working wives, especially working mothers, and assumed that only dire financial need excused it. Questions of status were involved, especially for working- and lower-middle-class families. A working wife cast doubts upon her husband's ability as a provider, and by extension on her own ability to attract a more competent mate. And the new Freudian ideas that swept through middle-class culture in the 1920s depicted career ambitions among women as compensations for unsatisfactory sex lives. The normal woman was not "restless" but was content in domesticity and maternity, especially since more modern attitudes toward sexual pleasure now allowed her to enjoy sex without guilt.

Women were also becoming disillusioned with their career prospects. At the beginning of the decade feminists were still convinced that the world of interesting work was opening before young women. The feminist Catherine Filene in 1920 produced a guidebook for women high school and college graduates, *Careers for Women*, which is remarkable in the sheer variety of jobs described, including selling life insurance ("if you are a real salesman you can be dropped from an airplane in any civilized locality and earn your living"); movie director ("the fact that there are only two women directors of note in the field today leaves an absolutely open field"); and private detective ("the qualifications necessary are absolute fearlessness ... initiative ... and patience"). No doubt a few young graduates did try all of these, but the majority continued to flock into the established "female" professions and jobs.

A notable statistic by 1920 was that the proportion of the female labor force that was white and native-born had increased from 52 percent in 1910 to more than 68 percent by 1920, largely due to the expansion of white-collar work, which now occupied more than 39 percent of women workers. The numbers of professional women and women in business increased during the 1920s, but not by huge numbers. In 1920, for example, there were 41 female engineers, but by 1930 still only 113; the number of women lawyers doubled between 1920 and 1930, but they still made up only 2 percent of the profession. And women found, as the pioneers at the beginning of the century had found, that their prospects for advancement were distinctly limited. Part of the "What Went Wrong?" style of journalism was devoted to examining why women were not making the rapid advances to the top that had been expected.

The *Journal* of the National Federation of Business and Professional Women conducted a running discussion from 1927 through 1929, trying to find explanations for women's slow progress and the limits on their achievement. Most contributors blamed it on gender discrimination and complained bitterly that women had to work twice as hard for the same recognition as a man. But many commentators were quick to blame women themselves for their lackluster performance.

The social scientist Lorine Pruette pointed to what she called "the stenographic attitude," a modesty of expectations that was really a form of cowardice. "Most women still lead contingent lives. . . . This is not so self-sacrificing; generally it appears to be the easier way." What most women still looked for, even in the world of work, was "the rewards of pleasing some other person. If women could get over the necessity of being pleasing, one very great obstacle to their success would be removed. . . ." The habits of mind and behavior bred for family and social success had not yet been sufficiently adapted to the somewhat different require-

ments of the more impersonal world of the job. A businesswoman dissecting in *Harper's* the "Seven Deadly Sins of Woman
in Business" thought the problem was that women had not
learned to read the male culture of the business world in which
they now found themselves. Relentlessly efficient, they had failed
to realize that success came as much from being able to trade gossip at the water cooler as in hard work and competence. Others
lamented the lack of support among women and the apparent
reluctance of women to work for other women. Many just felt
individually guilty because they had not fulfilled the personal
and cultural expectations of their youth: "Viewing my actual experience I realize how little I have played the role of the new
woman my friends and I talked so much about ten years ago,"
confessed one woman.

The new cultural importance of "psychologizing" as the mode
of understanding experience is evident in an interesting series of
essays in *The Nation* in 1926. The magazine's editor, Freda
Kirchwey, invited seventeen successful modern women who had
been notable feminists to discuss, anonymously, their feminism
and its origins. And then she brought in three psychologists to
comment upon their revelations. The assumption was that their
feminism was best explained by their personal experience, especially their childhood, rather than by wider social forces.

None of the women, who included Crystal Eastman, Inez
Haynes Irwin, and several other members of Heterodoxy, repudiated their feminism, though all wrote in somewhat ironic tones
of their necessary compromises. The modern reader is more
likely to be struck with the commentary of the "experts." John
Collier, a neurologist, pointing to the biblical command to "be
fruitful and multiply," lamented that "the woman who is willing
to have ten or twenty children is almost extinct," while men had
certainly been keeping up their end by determinedly "subduing
the earth." John B. Watson, a behavioral psychologist, saw the
new woman as a predatory creature who was out to rob men, "to
work at men's trades, to take men's jobs away from them, to get

men's salaries." Feminists were women who had failed to make a "sex adjustment." He discriminated among the seventeen essayists largely on the basis of which ones he would have liked to date. The sole woman commentator was Beatrice Hinkle, a pioneer Jungian psychoanalyst, who found the women's attitudes a "normal protest against external collective restrictions" but added that all of them exhibited weakness "on the side of their woman's nature."

By the end of the decade, several women were rethinking the possibilities and limits of individualism and were urging women once more toward some sort of renewed solidarity. Emily Newell Blair, in her "Wanted—a New Feminism," of 1930, said her experience in politics had convinced her that "only as we organize as women, work as women, and stand behind women, not only in politics, but everywhere, will we make ourselves a real force." Beatrice Hinkle thought she could already see a growing realization, emerging out of the very awakening of women as individuals, that "only in solidarity can any permanent impression be made on the old conception of woman as an inferior, dependent creature, useful for one purpose only." That renewed solidarity would have to wait, however, until the late 1960s, when the growing expectations for freedom and advancement—in the face of persistent cultural attitudes and institutional roadblocks—inspired collective action once more.

During the twenties, what one might describe as a new postsuffrage settlement was being worked out. Because of the abnormal circumstances of first the depression and then World War II, it did not reach its fullest realization until the 1950s. After the revolutionary upheavals of the late eighteenth century, the doctrine of "separate spheres" had represented a settlement of the relation of the sexes. It avoided sexual competition and preserved male superiority and control while placing less emphasis on the absolute inferiority of women and providing a certain degree of autonomy in the domestic sphere. The new settlement of the 1920s was more in tune with the economic developments of the preceding fifty years, which made it less useful to confine most women so completely to domesticity.

The new dispensation reflected and allowed women's greater economic utility and flexibility. This was due in great part to the fact that women in general were much better educated than in the past. At the end of the nineteenth century the president of the University of California at Berkeley had warned women undergraduates that they were not in college to be made into spinster schoolmarms but into more *serviceable* wives and mothers. One might say that by the 1920s women had become more serviceable in general. Daughters were no longer such financial drains on their fathers, nor unmarried mature women on their relations. Moreover they could fill a number of economic and social functions that society now found desirable to support, but at a moderate price, like universal public schooling, nursing care, and various social services. At the same time the dominance of husbands was maintained, though in a less obviously patriarchal fashion, by the fact that most wives, most of the time, did not work outside the home and thus depended economically on their husbands after marriage. Still, the utility of the housewife to the family was increased by the fact that she could work and bring in money in case of need.

The new dispensation now included formal equality of citizenship for women and a much greater degree of social freedom than in previous eras. It did not really disturb the ultimate dominance and control of men in politics or the economy, but it did provide, as all long-lasting colonial regimes learn to do, a few openings near the top for the exceptionally talented, determined, and ambitious of the subaltern class, thus drawing off possible sources of discontent and rebellion, just as the availability and declining stigma of divorce, and the availability of contraception, provided safety valves for the tensions of domesticity.

One might cite the automobile etiquette that began to develop in the 1920s as emblematic of the new gender arrangement. Part of the new "serviceability" of women was that they were more autonomously mobile: they could take commuter husbands to the train station and drive themselves on housewifely errands during the day. But when husbands and wives traveled together, the husband was expected to be firmly at the wheel. Or perhaps a better analogy might be the pattern in ballroom dancing, the dominant dance mode until the 1960s: men and women danced together in close contact as "partners," but the man led, the woman followed.

Like all good settlements, this one endured for some time because it had much to offer, both to men and women. When it eventually broke down, it was probably due to the rising expectations of women and the fact that due to their higher educational levels too many found themselves overqualified for the kinds of domestic tasks they spent much of their life doing. As the educational and general "competence gap" between men and women narrowed, the actual discrepancy in the tasks and roles they were expected to fulfill became more glaring and more galling. Individual female resentment simmered to the point where it could once again form the basis for a collective movement.

# 7

# The Fate of the ERA

THE OPPOSITION of the concerted forces of the Women's and Children's bureaus in the federal government, the union movement, and almost all of "organized womanhood" effectively stalled the equal-rights amendment in Congress. Although it was ritually reintroduced into every session of Congress after 1923, and in the 1940s both major parties gave it formal support in their platforms, it was not until the revival of feminism in the late 1960s that it had any real possibility of going through.

The new woman's movement, led by the National Organization for Women (NOW), made passage of the ERA a symbol of their struggle. Labor abandoned its opposition, since by now it was unlikely that the amendment would threaten to destroy protective labor legislation, and many women's business and professional groups joined in support. In 1972 the amendment sailed fairly easily through both houses of Congress and went to the states for ratification. So sure was practically everyone of ratification that at least one college textbook in American history printed it in its list of constitutional amendments in the back of the book. In the first year, twenty-two states ratified; but then the pace slowed as unexpected grass-roots opposition began to organize.

As in the early 1920s, the major battle was among women, but not this time *within* the feminist community. Led by Phyllis Schlafly, the opponents now were not women on the left who

feared for the well-being of the working woman, but largely
women on the right who were offended by a revived feminism
and who feared the loss of traditional "protections" such as a
guarantee of spousal support and alimony, and exemption from
military duty. Schlafly warned them that equal rights could be
used to legalize homosexual marriage and abortion. The result
was that politicians who had rather routinely responded to the
forces of feminism now equally routinely responded to their opponents. State legislatures now hesitated to endorse the ERA,
and Illinois went so far as to rescind its previous ratification. By
1977 the amendment was still three states shy of ratification, and
time was running out. Although Congress granted an extension
of time until July 1982, no additional states could be won over,
and the amendment failed. To many it seemed a fitting indication that feminism, after its spectacular resuscitation, had died
once more.

Yet the amendment has continued to be reintroduced in Congress in every session since 1982, and there are active if low-key
lobbies for it in most states. Proponents argue that the amendment would protect women against legislation or an unfriendly
Supreme Court that might attempt to roll back some of the gains
that women have made since the 1960s. Others insist that because
of those gains the ERA is now unnecessary. To some, what is
important is not so much practical results but enshrining the
idea of gender equality in the nation's central document. "It isn't
concrete, not something you can see will immediately help me in
my lifetime," said one activist. "It's more the principle of the
thing."

Which may be the problem. "Equality" is not a word or a concept that brings the same automatic endorsement as "liberty,"
and in spite of the Declaration of Independence it does not enjoy
quite the same status in the American pantheon of values. People
are not quite sure exactly what equality means or what it might
entail. And feminists themselves have been just as conflicted
about its meaning. Over the last century and a half, women have

gained many specific "equality" rights, and may gain more, but enshrining the concept of gender equality in the sacred text itself may prove too revolutionary.

# A Note on Sources

*General Works*

An indispensable reference work is Edward T. James, ed., *Notable American Women: A Biographical Dictionary, 1607–1950*, 3 vols. (Cambridge, Mass., 1971), and the succeeding volume, *Notable American Women: The Modern Period*, ed. Barbara Sicherman and Carol Hurd Green (Cambridge, Mass., 1980), which includes women who died between 1951 and 1976. A number of document collections are devoted to the suffrage and general women's rights movement. Among the best are Elizabeth Frost Knappman and Kathryn Cullen-DuPont, *Women's Suffrage in America: An Eyewitness History* (New York, 1992); Ruth Barnes Moynihan, et al., eds., *Second to None: A Documentary History of American Women*, 2 vols. (Lincoln, Nebr., 1993); and Sonya Michel and Robyn Muncy, eds., *Engendering America: A Documentary History, 1865 to the Present* (Boston, 1999). An invaluable resource which conveniently gathers many of the most important articles in women's history and groups them under general headings, such as "Politics," is Nancy F. Cott, ed., *History of Women in the United States: Historical Articles on Women's Lives and Activities* (New York, 1992ff), which has by now reached twenty volumes.

Among the best overview histories of American women are Nancy Woloch, *Women and the American Experience* (2nd ed., New York, 1994); Sara M. Evans, *Born for Liberty: A History of Women in America* (New York, 1989); and Sheila M. Rothman, *Woman's Proper Place: A History of Changing Ideals and Practices, 1870 to the Present* (New York, 1978). Rosalind Rosenberg, *Divided Lives: American Women in the Twentieth Century* (New York, 1992), and William H. Chafe, *The Paradox of Change: American Women in the 20th Century*

(New York, 1991) are both splendid interpretive overviews of the situation of women in the twentieth century. Nancy F. Cott, ed., *No Small Courage: A History of Women in the United States* (New York, 2000), has two chapters, by Harriet Sigerman and Karen Manners Smith, devoted to the period under discussion here. Nancy F. Cott's classic, *The Grounding of Modern Feminism* (New Haven, 1987), ranges widely from the 1890s through the 1920s. Christine Bolt, *The Women's Movements in the United States and Britain from the 1790s to the 1920s* (Amherst, Mass., 1993), is comprehensive and provides a valuable international perspective, as does Donald Meyer's more opinionated *Sex and Power: The Rise of Women in America, Russia, Sweden, and Italy* (Middletown, Conn., 1987). Peter G. Filene, *Him/Her/Self: Gender Identities in Modern America*, 3rd updated ed. (Baltimore, 1998), is a pioneering work in gender history (first published in 1975), which is still fresh and filled with insights. Rita Felski, *The Gender of Modernity* (Cambridge, Mass., 1995), is a fascinating discussion of early-twentieth-century feminist placing of selves within "the tradition of modernity." Margaret Gibbons Wilson, *The American Woman in Transition: The Urban Influence, 1870–1920* (Westport, Conn., 1979), is an interesting interpretive survey based on statistics.

In this book I refer frequently to several works by feminists of the period that make good reading: Rheta Childe Dorr, *A Woman of Fifty* (New York, 1924; reprinted New York, 1980); Olive Schreiner, *Woman and Labor* (New York, 1911); Katharine Anthony, *Feminism in Germany and Scandinavia* (New York, 1915); Lydia Kingsmill Commander, *The American Idea* (New York, 1972; orig. 1907); Catherine Filene, *Careers for Women* (Boston, 1920); Kate Gannett Wells, "The Transitional American Woman," *Atlantic Monthly* 46 (December 1880), 817–823; and Marlene Springer and Haskell Springer, eds., *Plains Woman: The Diary of Martha Farnsworth, 1882–1922* (Bloomington, Ind., 1986). The journalism of Crystal Eastman is conveniently collected in Blanche Wiesen Cook, ed., *Crystal Eastman on Women and Revolution* (New York, 1978). Elizabeth Stuart Phelps's novel about an early career woman, *Doctor Zay* (1882), is reprinted with an introduction by Michael Sartisky (New

York, 1987). Elsie Clews Parsons, *The Journal of a Feminist*, written
c. 1914, was published for the first time in 1994 (Newcastle-upon-
Tyne, U.K.) with an Introduction by Margaret C. Jones.


*Chapter 1. The Woman's Era*

See Emily Wortis Leider, *California's Daughter: Gertrude Atherton
and Her Times* (Stanford, Calif., 1991), for Atherton's assessment of
the "restless" woman.

Among many excellent works on women and higher education
at the turn of the century, see especially Barbara Miller Solomon, *In
the Company of Educated Women* (New Haven, 1985); several essays
by Lynn Gordon: "The Gibson Girl Goes to College: Popular Culture and Women's Higher Education in the Progressive Era,
1890–1920," *American Quarterly* 39 (Summer 1987); "Coeducation
on Two Campuses: Berkeley and Chicago, 1890–1912," in Carol
Lasser, ed., *Educating Men and Women Together* (Urbana, 1987); and
in the same volume, Patricia A. Palmieri, "From Republican Motherhood to Race Suicide: Arguments on the Higher Education of
Women in the United States, 1820–1920." See also Charlotte
Williams Conable, *Women at Cornell: The Myth of Equal Education*
(Ithaca, 1977); Joyce Antler, "'After College, What?' New Graduates and the Family Claim," *American Quarterly* 32 (Fall 1980),
409–434; Joan G. Zimmerman, "Daughters of Main Street: Culture
and the Female Community at Grinnell, 1884–1917," in Mary Kelley, ed., *Woman's Being, Woman's Place: Female Identity and Vocation
in American History* (Boston, 1979), 171–193; Lynn Gordon, *Gender
and Higher Education in the Progressive Era* (New Haven, 1990).

On the women's clubs, the classic account is Karen J. Blair, *The
Clubwoman as Feminist: True Womanhood Redefined, 1868–1914*
(New York, 1980). But two others that give full appreciation to the
emancipatory potential of the pure study club are Theodora Penny
Martin, *The Sound of Our Own Voices: Women's Study Clubs
1860–1910* (Boston, 1987); and Anne Ruggles Gere, *Intimate Practices: Literary and Cultural Work in U.S. Women's Clubs, 1880–1920*

(Urbana, 1997). Sandra Haarsager's *Organized Womanhood: Cultural Politics in the Pacific Northwest, 1840–1920* (Norman, Okla., 1997), is a wide-ranging discussion of women's roles in a neglected region. Joanne Reigano, "Working Girls Unite," *American Quarterly* 36, no. 1 (Spring 1984), 112–134, discusses the working girls' clubs.

The missionary enterprise is not usually given much space in general women's histories. One of the few historians to do so is Page Smith in *Daughters of the Promised Land, Women in American History* (Boston, 1970). Two excellent specialized studies are Patricia R. Hill, *The World Their Household: The American Woman's Foreign Mission Movement and Cultural Transformation, 1870–1920* (Ann Arbor, 1985); and Jane Hunter, *The Gospel of Gentility: American Women Missionaries in Turn-of-the-Century China* (New Haven, 1984). For New Thought, see Beryl Satter, *Each Mind a Kingdom: American Women, Sexual Purity, and the New Thought Movement, 1875–1920* (Berkeley, 1999).

There is much good scholarship on the Women's Christian Temperance Union. See, in particular, Ruth Bordin, *Frances Willard: A Biography* (Chapel Hill, 1986), and her *Woman and Temperance: The Quest for Power and Liberty, 1873–1900* (New Brunswick, N.J., 1990); and Jack S. Blocker, Jr., *American Temperance Movements: Cycles of Reform* (Boston, 1989). Willard's own *Writing Out My Heart: Selections from the Journal of Frances E. Willard, 1855–96,* with an Introduction by Carolyn De Swarte Gifford (Urbana, 1995), is interesting. On censorship, see Alison M. Parker, *Purifying America: Women, Cultural Reform, and Pro-Censorship Activism, 1873–1933* (Urbana, 1997); and for the crusade against prostitution, see David J. Pivar, *Purity Crusade: Sexual Morality and Social Control, 1868–1900* (Westport, Conn., 1973). For the international organization of women, see Leila J. Rupp, *Worlds of Women: The Making of an International Women's Movement* (Princeton, 1997); and Patricia Ward d'Itri, *Cross Currents in the International Women's Movement, 1848–1948* (Bowling Green, Ohio, 1999).

Several good essays on women in public life appear in Alison M. Parker and Stephanie Cole, eds., *Women and the Unstable State in*

*Nineteenth-Century America* (College Station, Tex., 2000). For the
women's movement in the last quarter of the century, Steven M.
Buechler, *The Transformation of the Woman Suffrage Movement: The
Case of Illinois, 1850–1920* (New Brunswick, N.J., 1986), is excellent.
Elizabeth Cady Stanton, Susan B. Anthony, and Matilda Joslyn
Gage, *History of Woman Suffrage*, 6 vols. (New York, 1881–1922;
reprinted Salem, N.H., 1985), is worth dipping into; Mari Jo and
Paul Buhle have edited this down to a one-volume *Concise History
of Woman Suffrage* (Urbana, 1978). Two good biographies of Eliza-
beth Cady Stanton are Elisabeth Griffith, *In Her Own Right: The
Life of Elizabeth Cady Stanton* (New York, 1984), and Lois W. Banner, *Elizabeth Cady Stanton, A Radical for Woman's Rights* (Boston,
1980). For Susan B. Anthony, see Kathleen Barry, *Susan B. Anthony:
A Biography of a Singular Feminist* (New York, 1988); the older Ida
Husted Harper, *Life and Work of Susan B. Anthony,* 3 vols. (Indi-
anapolis, 1898–1908; reprinted Salem, N.H., 1983), contains copies
of no longer extant letters and some of Anthony's speeches. Ellen C.
DuBois, ed. and Introduction, *Elizabeth Cady Stanton, Susan B. Anthony: Correspondence, Writings, Speeches* (rev. ed., New York, 1992),
is indispensable; the volume contains Stanton's "Solitude of Self"
speech and extracts from some of the letters sent to Anthony about
the vote. For Julia Ward Howe, see Deborah P. Clifford, *Mine Eyes
Have Seen the Glory: A Biography of Julia Ward Howe* (Boston, 1979).
Katherine Devereux Blake and Margaret Louise Wallace, *Champion of Women: The Life of Lillie Devereux Blake* (New York, 1943),
is a biography of a lesser-known suffragist by her daughter.
Mary A. Livermore, *The Story of My Life* (Hartford, Conn., 1897).
For the women's rights press, see Martha M. Solomon,
*A Voice of Their Own: The Woman Suffrage Press, 1840–1910*
(Tuscaloosa, Ala., 1991). For Chicago's Columbian Exposition of
1893, see Robert Muccigrosso, *Celebrating the New World* (Chicago,
1993). The fullest treatment of women and the fair is Jeanne Made-
line Weimann, *The Fair Women* (Chicago, 1981). My discussion of
Mary Cassatt's mural comes from John Hutton, "Picking Fruit:
Mary Cassatt's 'Modern Woman' and the Woman's Building of

1893," *Feminist Studies* 20, no. 2 (Summer 1994), 319–348. The speeches of African-American women at the Chicago fair can be conveniently found at the "Women and Social Movements in the United States, 1775–2000" section of the woman's history project at Binghamton University website: http://womhist.binghamton.edu/ibw/doclist.htm.

## Chapter 2. The New Woman and the New Politics

On many aspects of female activism, a particularly valuable collection of essays is Nancy A. Hewitt and Suzanne Lebsock, eds., *Visible Women: New Essays on American Activism* (Urbana, 1993). Barbara Kuhn Campbell, *The "Liberated" Woman of 1914: Prominent Women in the Progressive Era* (Ann Arbor, 1979), is an analysis of the characteristics of the nine thousand women who appeared in *Woman's Who's Who of America,* published in 1914; Dorothy Schneider and Carl J. Schneider, *American Women in the Progressive Era, 1900–1920* (New York, 1993), is a lively and wide-ranging account of the myriad changes taking place in women's lives in the early twentieth century.

On women and the professions, see Penina Migdal Glazer and Miriam Slater, *Unequal Colleagues: The Entrance of Women into the Professions, 1890–1940* (New Brunswick, N.J., 1987), and Joyce Antler, *The Educated Woman and Professionalization: The Struggle for a New Feminine Identity, 1890–1920* (New York, 1987). For problems of career for the educated woman, see Patricia A. Palmieri, "The Simplest of New England Spinsters": Becoming Emily Greene Balch, 1867–1961," in Susan L. Porter, ed., *Women of the Commonwealth* (Amherst, Mass., 1996), and Antler, " 'After College, What?' "

For home economics, see Sarah Stage, "Ellen Richards and the Social Significance of the Home Economics Movement," in Sarah Stage, ed., *Rethinking Home Economics* (Ithaca, 1997), 17–33.

In an extensive literature on women doctors, see especially Mary Roth Walsh, *"Doctors Wanted, No Women Need Apply": Sexual Barriers in the Medical Profession, 1835–1975* (New Haven, 1977); and

Regina Markell Morantz-Sanchez, *Sympathy and Science: Women Physicians in American Medicine* (New York, 1985). For nursing and nurses' relation to the woman movement, see Sandra Beth Lewenson, *Taking Charge: Nursing, Suffrage and Feminism in America, 1873–1920* (New York, 1993). For women in science, the best source is Margaret W. Rossiter, *Women Scientists in America: Struggles and Strategies to 1940* (Baltimore, 1982); on Alice Hamilton, see Barbara Sicherman, *Alice Hamilton, A Life in Letters* (Cambridge, Mass., 1984). Also Regina Markell Morantz, "Feminism, Professionalism, and Germs: The Thought of Mary Putnam Jacobi and Elizabeth Blackwell," *American Quarterly* 34 (Winter 1982), 459–478.

On the "Bachelor Woman," see "Bachelor Girls in New York," *Scribners,* 1896. G. Stanley Hall on the "Bachelor Woman" is in Susan Groag Bell and Karen M. Offen, *Women, the Family, and Freedom: The Debate in Documents* (Stanford, Calif., 1983), II, 157–163.

For the growth of white-collar work for women, see Elyse Rotella, *From Home to Office: U.S. Women at Work, 1870–1930* (Ann Arbor, 1981); Margery W. Davies, *Woman's Place Is at the Typewriter: Office Work and Office Workers, 1870–1930* (Philadelphia, 1982); Sharon Hartman Strom, *Beyond the Typewriter: Gender, Class, and the Origins of Modern Office Work, 1900–1930*; and Lisa M. Fine, *The Souls of the Skyscraper: Female Clerical Workers in Chicago, 1870–1930* (Philadelphia, 1990).

There is an extensive literature on women and progressive reform. For the settlement houses, see Allen F. Davis, *Spearheads for Reform* (New York, 1967); Roy Lubove, *The Professional Altruist: The Emergence of Social Work as a Career, 1880–1930* (Cambridge, Mass., 1965); and Robyn Muncy, *Creating a Female Dominion in American Reform, 1890–1935* (New York, 1991).

An excellent and thought-provoking overview of much of the recent literature on "maternalist" reform and the origins of the American welfare state is Patrick Wilkinson, "The Selfless and the Helpless: Maternalist Origins of the U.S. Welfare State," *Feminist Studies* 25, no. 3 (Fall 1999), 571–597. The early career of Florence Kelley is examined in Kathryn Kish Sklar, *Florence Kelley and the*

*Nation's Work: The Rise of Women's Political Culture, 1830–1900*
(New Haven, 1995). The best sources for women and the mothers'
pension movement are Sklar, "The Historical Foundations of
Women's Power in the Creation of the American Welfare State
1830–1930," in Seth Koven and Sonya Michel, eds., *Mothers of a
New World: Maternalist Politics and the Origins of Welfare States*
(New York, 1993); and Theda Skocpol, *Protecting Soldiers and Moth-
ers: The Political Origins of Social Policy in the United States* (Cam-
bridge, Mass., 1992). For protective hours and wages legislation, see
Vivien Hart, *Bound by Our Constitution: Women, Workers and the
Minimum Wage* (Princeton, 1994); and Alice Kessler Harris, *A
Woman's Wage: Historical Meanings and Social Consequences* (Lexing-
ton, Ky., 1990), and her *In Pursuit of Equity: Women, Men and the
Quest for Economic Citizenship in 20th-Century America* (New York,
2001). Sybil Lipschultz, "Hours and Wages: The Gendering of
Labor Standards in America," *Journal of Women's History* 8 (Spring
1996); 114–136, is an insightful essay on the question of "rights" versus "needs." Ulla Wikander, Alice Kessler-Harris, and Jane Lewis,
eds., *Protecting Women: Labor Legislation in Europe, the United
States, and Australia, 1880–1920* (Urbana, 1995), shows the international dimension of the question of protective legislation for
women.

On the WTUL, see Robin Miller Jacoby, "The Women's Trade
Union League and American Feminism," *Feminist Studies* 3, no. 1/2
(Fall 1975), 126–140; and Nancy Schrom Dye, *As Equals and as Sis-
ters: Feminism, the Labor Movement, and the Women's Trade Union
League of New York* (Columbia, Mo., 1980). For working girls and
"finery," see Nan Enstad, *Ladies of Labor, Girls of Adventure: Work-
ing Women, Popular Culture, and Labor Politics at the Turn of the
Twentieth Century* (New York, 1999).

*Chapter 3. Thinking About the Woman Question*

The recovery of Matilda Joslyn Gage is owed mainly to the work of
Sally Roesch Wagner. See her Introduction to the reprint of Gage's
*Woman, Church, and State* (Watertown, Mass., 1980; orig. 1893). The

modern feminist Mary Daly makes use of Gage's ideas in *Gyn/Ecol-ogy* (Boston, 1978). There is a recent biography: Leila R. Brammer, *Excluded from Suffrage History: Matilda Joslyn Gage, Nineteenth-Century American Feminist* (Westport, Conn., 2000); and see also Dale Spender, *Women of Ideas and What Men Have Done to Them* (London, 1982). Kathi Kern, *Mrs. Stanton's Bible* (Ithaca, 2001), is a superb, wide-ranging account of the religious ideas of Elizabeth Cady Stanton and many of her colleagues, the writing of the Woman's Bible, and the reactions to it. The Woman's Bible has been reissued: Elizabeth Cady Stanton, *The Woman's Bible* (Boston, 1993; orig. 1895), with a Foreword by Maureen Fitzgerald.

For evolutionary ideas and their impact on women, see Cynthia Eagle Russett, *Sexual Science: The Victorian Construction of Woman-hood* (Cambridge, Mass., 1989); Lorna Duffin, "Prisoners of Progress: Women and Evolution," in Sara Delamont and Lorna Duffin, eds., *The Nineteenth-Century Woman: Her Cultural and Physical World* (London, 1978), 57–91; Jill Conway, "Stereotypes of Femininity in a Theory of Sexual Evolution," *Victorian Studies* 14 (September 1970), 47–62; Elizabeth Fee, "Science and the Woman Problem: Historical Perspectives," in Michael S. Teitelbaum, ed., *Sex Differences: Social and Biological Perspectives* (Garden City, N.Y., 1976), and Fee, "The Sexual Politics of Victorian Anthropology," in Mary S. Hartman and Lois Banner, eds., *Clio's Consciousness Raised: New Perspectives on the History of Women* (New York, 1974). Antoinette Brown Blackwell and Darwin are discussed in Marie Tedesco, "A Feminist Challenge to Darwinism: Antoinette L. B. Blackwell on the Relations of the Sexes in Nature and Society," in Diane L. Fowlkes and Charlotte S. McClure, eds., *Feminist Visions* (University, Ala., 1984); and Elizabeth Munson and Greg Dickinson, "Hearing Women Speak: Antoinette Brown Blackwell and the Dilemma of Authority," *Journal of Women's History* 10, no. 1 (Spring 1998). A fascinating collection of documents is Louise M. Newman, ed., *Men's Ideas/Women's Realities* (New York, 1985), drawn from the *Popular Science Monthly*. The mixture of commentary and docu-ments in Elizabeth K. Helsinger, Robin Lauterbach Sheets, and William Veeder, eds., *The Woman Question: Society and Literature in*

*Britain and America, 1837–1883* (New York, 1983), vol. 2, is also interesting, especially on Antoinette Blackwell.

There is now an extensive body of work on Charlotte Perkins Gilman. I relied most heavily on the following: Larry Ceplair, ed., *Charlotte Perkins Gilman: A Nonfiction Reader* (New York, 1991); Jill Rudd and Val Gough, eds., *Charlotte Perkins Gilman: Optimist Reformer* (Iowa City, 1999); Jane S. Upin, "Charlotte Perkins Gilman: Instrumentalism Beyond Dewey," *Hypatia* 8, no. 2 (Spring 1993), 38–59; and Brian Lloyd, "Feminism, Utopian and Scientific: Charlotte Perkins Gilman and the Prison of the Familiar," *American Studies* 39 (Spring 1998), 93–113. Recently more critical feminists have noted the centrality of racism in Gilman's thinking, as with women reformers and suffragists more generally. See particularly Louise M. Newman, *White Women's Rights: The Racial Origins of Feminism in the United States* (New York, 1999). Gail Bederman devotes a chapter to Gilman's racism in *Manliness and Civilization: A Cultural History of Gender and Race in the United States, 1880–1917* (Chicago, 1995). Alys Eve Weinbaum, "Writing Feminist Genealogy: Charlotte Perkins Gilman, Racial Nationalism, and the Reproduction of Maternalist Feminism," *Feminist Studies* 27, no. 2 (Summer 2001), 271–302, also insists on the centrality of a racist evolutionism to Gilman's thought. Several writers explicate the evolutionary strains of her thought, especially Bernice L. Hausman, "Sex Before Gender: Charlotte Perkins Gilman and the Evolutionary Paradigm of Utopia," *Feminist Studies* 24, no. 3 (Fall 1998), 489–510. Biographies of Gilman include Ann J. Lane, *To Herland and Beyond: The Life and Work of Charlotte Perkins Gilman* (New York, 1990), and for her early life, Mary A. Hill, *Charlotte Perkins Gilman: The Making of a Radical Feminist, 1860–1896* (Philadelphia, 1980). The most readily available of Gilman's own works are *Women and Economics: The Economic Relation Between Men and Women as a Factor in Social Evolution* (New York, 1966; orig. 1898), with an Introduction by Carl Degler; the utopian novel *Herland* in *Herland, the Yellow Wall-Paper, and Selected Writings,* ed. Denise D. Knight (New York, 1999); and her autobiography, *The Living of Charlotte*

*Perkins Gilman* (1935, reprinted New York, 1975), with an Introduction by Zona Gale.

For the importance of the work ethic to feminism, especially to Gilman and Olive Schreiner, see Daniel T. Rodgers, *The Work Ethic in Industrial America, 1850–1920* (Chicago, 1978).

On social science and ideas about women, I have relied most heavily on Rosalind Rosenberg, *Beyond Separate Spheres: Intellectual Roots of Modern Feminism* (New Haven, 1982); Rosenberg, "The Academic Prism: The New View of American Women," in Carol Ruth Berkin and Mary Beth Norton, *Women of America: A History* (Boston, 1979), 319–341; Helene Silverberg, ed., *Gender and American Social Science: The Formative Years* (Princeton, 1998); and James Livingston, "The Strange Career of the 'Social Self,'" *Radical History Review* 76 (Winter 2000), 53–79. For the problem of the family, see Ann Taylor Allen, "Feminism, Social Science, and the Meanings of Modernity: The Debate on the Origin of the Family in Europe and the United States, 1860–1914," *American Historical Review* 104, no. 4 (October 1999), 1085–1113; and *American Journal of Sociology* 14, no. 6 (May 1909).

*Chapter 4. Feminism and the Problem of Sex*

On marriage and careers, see Joyce Antler, *Lucy Sprague Mitchell: The Making of a Modern Woman* (New Haven, 1987); and Frederic C. Howe, *The Confessions of a Reformer* (New York, 1925). The quotations from W. I. Thomas come from excerpts in Anne Firor Scott, ed., *The American Woman: Who Was She?* (Englewood Cliffs, N.J., 1971).

On Greenwich Village and bohemia, see June Sochen, *Movers and Shakers: American Women Thinkers and Activists, 1900–1970* (New York, 1973), and *The New Woman: Feminism in Greenwich Village, 1910–1920* (New York, 1972); Floyd Dell, *Woman as World Builders* (1913; reprinted Westport, Conn., 1976); and Christine Stansell's recent sophisticated account, *American Moderns: Bohemian New York and the Creation of a New Century* (New York, 2000). Ellen Kay

Trimberger, "Feminism, Men and Modern Love: Greenwich Village 1900–1925," in Ann Snitow, et al., eds., *Powers of Desire* (New York, 1983), 131–152, discusses some of the problems Villagers experienced in combining sexual desire, emotional intimacy, and marriage. See also her "The New Woman and the New Sexuality: Conflict and Contradiction in the Writings and Lives of Mabel Dodge and Neith Boyce," in Adele Heller and Lois Rudnick, eds., *1915: The Cultural Moment* (New Brunswick, N.J., 1991); and Kate Wittenstein, "The Feminist Uses of Psychoanalysis: Beatrice M. Hinkle and the Foreshadowing of Modern Feminism in the United States," *Journal of Women's History* 10, no. 2 (Summer 1998), 38–62. On prostitution, see Mark Thomas Connelly, *The Response to Prostitution in the Progressive Era* (Chapel Hill, 1980); and David J. Langum, *Crossing Over the Line: Legislating Morality and the Mann Act* (Chicago, 1994).

On sexual freedom in the early years of the century, see Elizabeth Wilson, *The Sphinx in the City: Urban Life, the Control of Disorder, and Women* (Berkeley, 1992); James R. McGovern, "The American Woman's Pre–World War I Freedom in Manners and Morals," *Journal of American History* 55 (September 1968), 315–333; and Lewis A. Erenberg, "Everybody's Doin' It: The Pre–World War I Dance Craze, The Castles, and the Modern American Girl," *Feminist Studies* 3, nos. 1, 2 (Fall 1975), 154–170, and *Steppin' Out: New York Nightlife and the Transformation of American Culture, 1890–1930* (Westport, Conn., 1981). Kevin White, *Sexual Liberation or Sexual License?: The American Revolt Against Victorianism* (Chicago, 2000), is a lively account of changing sexual mores.

On Heterodoxy, see Judith Schwartz, *Radical Feminists of Heterodoxy: Greenwich Village, 1912–1940* (Lebanon, N.H., 1982); and on Village radicalism, see Margaret C. Jones, *Heretics and Hellraisers: Women Contributors to "The Masses," 1911–1917* (Austin, Tex., 1993), and Leslie Fishbein, *Rebels in Bohemia: The Radicals of "The Masses," 1911–1917* (Chapel Hill, 1982). Also see Sandra Adickes, *To Be Young Was Very Heaven: Women in New York Before the First World War* (New York, 1997).

Desley Deacon, *Elsie Clews Parsons: Inventing Modern Life*

(Chicago, 1997), is an excellent biography of a lesser-known icono-
clastic feminist. For the new "togetherness," see Margaret Marsh,
"Suburban Men and Masculine Domesticity, 1870–1915," in Mark
C. Carnes and Clyde Griffen, eds., *Meanings for Manhood: Construc-
tions of Masculinity in Victorian America* (Chicago, 1990), 111–127.
For the birth-control movement, see Linda Gordon, *Woman's Body,
Woman's Right: A Social History of Birth Control in America* (New
York, 1976); Andrea Tone, *Devices and Desires: A History of Contraceptives in America* (New York, 2001); Carole R. McCann, *Birth Control Politics in the United States, 1916–1945* (Ithaca, 1994); and a good
summary article by James Reed, "The Birth-Control Movement Before Roe v. Wade," in Donald T. Critchlow, ed., *The Politics of Abortion and Birth Control in Historical Perspective* (University Park, Pa.,
1996). For Margaret Sanger, see David Kennedy's *Birth Control in
America: The Career of Margaret Sanger* (New Haven, 1970), and on
her rival for leadership of the movement, Mary Ware Dennett, see
Constance M. Chen, *The Sex Side of Life* (New York, 1996).


*Chapter 5. War and Victory*

Two classic and still pertinent overviews of the suffrage movement
are Eleanor Flexner, *Century of Struggle,* rev. ed. (Cambridge, Mass.,
1975), and Aileen S. Kraditor, *The Ideas of the Woman Suffrage
Movement, 1890–1920* (New York, 1965). Marjorie Spruill Wheeler,
ed., *One Woman, One Vote: Rediscovering the Woman Suffrage Movement* (Troutdale, Ore., 1995), is a splendid collection of modern essays which together offer a thorough overview of the suffrage
movement. It can be supplemented with Jean H. Baker, ed., *Votes
for Women: The Struggle for Suffrage Revisited* (New York, 2002).
Ellen Carol DuBois has made many valuable contributions to suffrage history over the last decade, not least in insisting on the importance of the struggle for the vote. I have relied most heavily on the
essays conveniently collected in *Woman Suffrage and Women's Rights*
(New York, 1998) and her biography of Elizabeth Cady Stanton's
daughter, *Harriot Stanton Blatch and the Winning of Woman Suffrage*
(New Haven, 1997). DuBois, ed., "Spanning Two Centuries: The

Autobiography of Nora Stanton Barney," *History Workshop Journal*
22 (Autumn 1986), is a delightful small piece by Cady Stanton's
granddaughter.

Other useful biographies of suffragists are Jacqueline Van Voris,
*Carrie Chapman Catt: A Public Life* (New York, 1987), and Sharon
Hartman Strom, *Political Woman: Florence Luscomb and the Legacy
of Radical Reform* (Philadelphia, 2001). Leila J. Rupp, "Is Feminism
the Province of Old (or Middle-Aged) Women?" *Journal of Women's
History* 12, no. 4 (Winter 2001), 164–173, discusses the age question
in feminism. Suzanne M. Marilley, *Woman Suffrage and the Origins
of Liberal Feminism in the United States, 1820–1920* (Cambridge,
Mass., 1996), is especially good on the last stages of the campaign
with its emphasis on the intensive lobbying of politicians. Sara
Hunter Graham, *Woman Suffrage and the New Democracy* (New
Haven, 1996), is a highly critical account of the tactics of the suf-
frage leaders in the final phase of the struggle. Christine A. Lunar-
dini, *From Equal Suffrage to Equal Rights: Alice Paul and the
National Woman's Party, 1910–1928* (New York, 1986), details the
importance of this wing of the suffrage movement, as does Linda G.
Ford, *Iron-Jawed Angels: The Suffrage Militancy of the National
Woman's Party, 1912–1920* (Lanham, Md., 1991). Sherna Gluck, ed.,
*From Parlor to Prison: Five American Suffragists Talk About Their
Lives* (New York, 1976), consists of fascinating interviews with five
"rank and file suffragists."

There are a number of fairly recent discussions of particular as-
pects of the final phases of the suffrage campaign: Margaret
Finnegan, *Selling Suffrage: Consumer Culture and Votes for Women*
(New York, 1999), gives a colorful account of the "advertising of
suffrage," and Virginia Scharff, *Taking the Wheel: Women and the
Coming of the Motor Age* (New York, 1991), deals both with the use
of cars in suffrage campaigns and with women drivers in World
War I.

Two interesting books on actresses as "New Women" and suffragists are Albert Auster, *Actresses and Suffragists: Women in the American Theater, 1890–1920* (New York, 1984), and Susan A. Glenn,

*Female Spectacle: The Theatrical Roots of Modern Feminism* (Cambridge, Mass., 2000). The often wary relationship between women and socialism is detailed in Mari Jo Buhle's classic account, *Women and American Socialism, 1870–1920* (Urbana, 1981). Sandra F. VanBurkleo, *"Belonging to the World": Women's Rights and American Constitutional Culture* (New York, 2001), is an extremely interesting discussion of women and their relationship to the "constitutional order."

Anti-suffragism has garnered some scholarly interest: see Jane Jerome Camhi, *Women Against Women: American Anti-Suffragism, 1880–1920* (Brooklyn, 1994), which has a good chapter on Ida Tarbell; and Susan E. Marshall, *Splintered Sisterhood: Gender and Class in the Campaign Against Woman Suffrage* (Madison, Wisc., 1997). State and local studies include Gayle Gullett, *Becoming Citizens: The Emergence and Development of the California Women's Movement, 1880–1911* (Urbana, 2000); Elinor Lerner, "Family Structure, Occupational Patterns, and Support for Women's Suffrage," in Judith Friedlander, et al., eds., *Women in Culture and Politics: A Century of Change* (Bloomington, Ind., 1986), 223–236; Elna C. Green, *Southern Strategies: Southern Women and the Woman Suffrage Question* (Chapel Hill, 1997); Louise R. Noun, *Strong-Minded Women: The Emergence of the Woman-Suffrage Movement in Iowa* (Ames, Iowa, 1969).

For African-American women as suffragists, and the racism in the NAWSA, see Rosalyn Terborg-Penn, *African American Women in the Struggle for the Vote, 1850–1920* (Bloomington, Ind., 1998); "The Historical Treatment of Afro-Americans in the Woman's Movement, 1900–1920: A Bibliographical Essay," in *A Current Bibliography on African Affairs* 7 (Summer 1974), 245–258, and in the same volume, Irene Diggs, "Du Bois and Women: a Short Story of Black Women, 1910–1934," 260–303; Patricia A. Schechter, *Ida B. Wells-Barnett and American Reform, 1880–1930* (Chapel Hill, 2001); Barbara Hilkert Andolsen, *"Daughters of Jefferson, Daughters of Bootblacks": Racism and American Feminism* (Macon, Ga., 1986); Nancie Caraway, *Segregated Sisterhood: Racism and the Politics of*

*American Feminism* (Knoxville, Tenn., 1991); Paula Giddings, *When and Where I Enter: The Impact of Black Women on Race and Sex in America* (New York, 1984); and Anna Julia Cooper, *A Voice from the South* (New York, 1988; orig. 1892).

Christine A. Lunardini and Thomas J. Knock, "Woodrow Wilson and Woman Suffrage: A New Look," *Political Science Quarterly* 95 (Winter 1980–1981), 655–671, details the crucial support of President Wilson; Carrie Chapman Catt and Nettie Rogers Shuler, *Woman Suffrage and Politics* (New York, 1923), is Catt's summing up of the last phases of the struggle.

For the role of women in World War I, see Maureen Weiner Greenwald, *Women, War, and Work: The Impact of World War I on Women Workers in the United States* (Westport, Conn., 1980).

## Chapter 6. After the Vote

Nancy F. Cott's *The Grounding of Modern Feminism* (New Haven, 1987), is the standard work on the emergence of a new "feminist consciousness" from the old suffrage movement. Dorothy M. Brown, *Setting a Course: American Women in the 1920s* (Boston, 1987), is an excellent survey of the decade. J. Stanley Lemons, in *The Woman Citizen: Social Feminism in the 1920s* (Urbana, 1973), was one of the first historians to draw attention to the significance of the Sheppard-Towner Act. Kristi Andersen, *After Suffrage: Women in Partisan Electoral Politics Before the New Deal* (Chicago, 1996), deals with women and the parties.

For the ERA and the bitter quarrels over it, see Amy E. Butler, *Two Paths to Equality: Alice Paul and Ethel M. Smith in the ERA Debate, 1921–1929* (New York, 2002), and Susan D. Becker, *The Origins of the Equal Rights Amendment* (Westport, Conn., 1981). Many of the books cited for Chapter 2 also deal with the ERA. Vivian Hart, for example, has a very good chapter in *Bound by Our Constitution* (Princeton, 1994).

*The Nation*'s series on "Modern Women" is reproduced in Elaine Showalter, ed., *These Modern Women: Autobiographical Essays from the Twenties* (rev. ed., New York, 1989). For the problems of professional women after 1920, see Patricia M. Hummer, *The Decade of Elusive Promise: Professional Women in the United States, 1920–1930* (Ann Arbor, UMI Research Press, 1979), and Virginia MacMakin Collier, *Marriage and Careers: A Study of One Hundred Women Who Are Wives, Mothers, Homemakers and Professional Workers* (New York, 1926). Angela Howard and Sasha R. A. Tarrant, eds., *Antifeminism in America* (New York, 2000), contains some of the oppositional writings of the decade. Robert Max Jackson, *Destined for Equality: The Inevitable Rise of Women's Status* (Cambridge, Mass., 1998), suggests that the equality of women is a natural concomitant of the rise of modern political and economic organization.

# Index

# A NOTE ON THE AUTHOR

Jean V. Matthews was born in London and studied at the University of London, Smith College, and Harvard University, where she received a Ph.D. in American history. She is the author of *Women's Struggle for Equality: The First Phase, 1828–1876*; *Rufus Choate: The Law and Civic Virtue*; and *Toward a New Society: American Thought and Culture, 1800–1830*. Ms. Matthews is professor emeritus at the University of Western Ontario, Canada, and now lives in Oakland, California.